BEYO

She

ILLUSTRATIONS
Harry Hawkins

A *Cyprus* **Mail**
BOOK

A Cyprus **Mail** Publication

First published in Cyprus in 1999 by
Cyprus Mail Co. Ltd.,
24 Vassiliou Voulgaroctonou,
P.O. Box 1144, Nicosia
Cyprus

ISBN 9963-8377-1-9

ACKNOWLEDGEMENTS

My thanks, as always, to Harry for his superb illustrations, to Rob Thompson for his support, and to my editor, Steve Myles, for his expertise and good humour when I bend the English language.

Sheila Hawkins, Neo Khorio, May 1999

By the same author

The Back of Beyond
Beyond Our Dreams

AUTHOR'S NOTE

To assist the flow of the narrative some events may not be portrayed in strict chronological order.

DEDICATION

For Harry, the other half of the team, with love.

CONTENTS

ILLUSTRATIONS

All illustrations by HARRY HAWKINS

Front Cover......Acrylic painting

Back Cover.......Oil painting
(from a photograph by Andreas Pistentis)

GLOSSARY

akanthochiros	hedgehog
anari	local cheese
bundu	waste ground
chapatti	pitta bread
eshis veloni, kori?	Have you a needle, daughter?
fetta	local cheese
flaounes	Cypriot Easter cakes
gazome	farewell party (slang)
gizzit	free car (slang)
glysteritha	edible salad plant
glühwein	spiced mulled wine
halloumi	local cheese
Ime poli arostos	I am very ill
janner	native of Devon (slang)
jellaba	Arab robe
junta	administrative faction
kafejis	coffee shop proprietor
kafeneion	coffee shop
kali mera	good morning
KD	khaki drill
kefalos	grey mullet
kokinelli	sweet red wine

kopiaste	come, share with me
koumpare	best man
loukanika	sausages
lounza	smoked pork loin
mandila	headscarf
markouji	flexible tube
mantra	sheepfold
metrios	Greek coffee (medium sweet)
moufflon	wild sheep
nargileh	hookah water pipe
O Theos mazi sou	may God be with you
orfos	grouper fish
ouzo	aniseed-flavoured liquor
Panayia	The Holy Virgin
piastre	old monetary unit
souvla	meat done over charcoal
tappas	digging tool
vraka	black baggy trousers
vrougalli	small hand brush
xenos	stranger
zivania	alcohol distilled from grapes
ziziros	cicada

The huge delta-winged bomber

1. IT STARTS HERE

The huge delta-winged bomber loomed out of the morning mist on its landing approach. The engines went into reverse thrust as it touched down and a deafening roar shook the house. The braking parachute deployed and the giant aircraft came to a halt close to the end of the runway. The Lincolnshire mist swirled in over the airfield, and like a pale phantom the aptly named Vulcan disappeared from view.

Standing at the window of our married quarter, which stood ear-bendingly near the runway, I thought of Harry squeezed into the seventh seat at the back and knew that, like the crew, he would be glad to be down after the near five-hour flight from Newfoundland. It was 1971, and tensions were high between east and west. The cold war prevailed, and the massive Vulcan bombers, together with the Royal Navy's Polaris submarines, were Britain's main deterrent against the nuclear threat from the Soviet Union.

The children, neat in their school uniforms, were spooning porridge at the kitchen table. Now they went into overdrive.

"Daddy's back, Daddy's back" they chanted. They pushed away their plates and chased each other around the room in excitement. When they came home for lunch, there would be something special for them in the familiar air force blue grip.

Soon the phone rang.

"Hold the coffee, love. The debrief's over but the Wing Commander wants to see me before I come home."

The children went off to school and I made a start on the routine household chores. Soon a landrover drove along Tedder Drive, dropping the tired fliers off. Harry was the first to jump down. I opened the front door and waved to the others as my husband dashed up the path grinning broadly and waving a piece of paper. He swept me off my feet and kissed me while the crew whistled and applauded.

I sensed something out of the ordinary had happened. The smile simply wouldn't come off his face. He wiggled the piece of paper.

"My posting's through. We go to Cyprus in August!"

* * * * *

The days of glamorous overseas postings were rapidly becoming a thing of the past. Many RAF officers were resigned to serving most of their time in the so-called Royal Lincolnshire Air Force. As it happened we had both enjoyed our first Lincolnshire tour. Harry was posted to the College of Air Warfare at Manby and we rented a delightful cottage at the invigorating seaside resort of Mablethorpe: miles and miles of golden sand with surf pounding up the beach and all the fresh air one could wish for. The following year, shortly before the birth of our second child, we moved into a bungalow at Sutton-on-Sea. It was an ideal environment in which to raise young children, and we have many happy memories of those days. We were not displeased, therefore, when a few years later we heard we were to return to Lincolnshire - attached to Bomber Group at RAF Waddington.

Those too were wonderful days. Harry loved his new job and, already a qualified swimming teacher, I was now presented with the opportunity to attend a full-time course in physical education in the nearby city of Lincoln. I studied the commitment carefully. On four days a week I would easily be home in time to fetch the children from school, but on the fifth day I would be required to attend for a full day. A close friend of mine, who also had two children, was just as keen to go to college. She wanted to study history, and as her full day would not coincide with mine, we quickly realised we could easily cover for each other. Once a week, we would have four children instead of two for the day.

We sent in our applications, passed the appropriate tests and, at the beginning of the autumn term, we enrolled as full-time mature students at Bishop Grosseteste College in Lincoln. I used to wonder what kind of a bishop he was with a name like that, but Josie assured me that the French tête used to be written as teste, so it appears he only had a big head. Formerly a college for young ladies, it now boasted men on most of the courses, but the physical education department was most definitely for women only. We were issued with our new gear: track suit, hockey shorts and sports sweater in the college's elegant dark green and various regulation sports shirts and underwear fashioned to match or tone with it all. My children were most impressed. They were used to seeing me in sports gear, but this was a proper uniform, complete with a long, striped scarf.

"Well," said Harry, wincing as he saw the amount on the cheque made out to the official sports outfitter in Leicester. "That's kitted you out, now all we need to do is get you your own car."

My own car! Not well off enough to be a two-car family, the words had a sweet ring to them. I could taste a big slice of freedom and independence coming my way. I imagined myself swanning around in something suitably sporty - even perhaps in a British racing green colour to go well with all my new clothes.

A few days later Harry came home saying he'd heard of an ideal small car to get me the few miles to college and back every day. We would take a look at it that evening. There was no way the kids were going to be left out of this adventure, so at six o'clock we found ourselves standing outside a house in a nearby village. A man answered our knock at the door.

"You must be Harry Hawkins. It's round the back."

We trooped round the back to a run-down looking piece of waste ground. There were oil drums, old engines, worn-out tyres and a couple of large sheets of plastic among various other bits and pieces left lying around. I couldn't see a car - sporty, gleaming or otherwise.

The man moved across to one of the large sheets of plastic and pulled it to one side. I found myself looking at a small round object with wheels. It was covered in grime and didn't appear to be much larger than our chest freezer.

Jeremy dived forward. "It's a toy car, Mummy," he said joyfully.

"This is no toy, son," said the man. "*This* is an Isetta." And so began my love affair with a bubble-car.

* * * * *

Harry brought the tiny car back to the base and lovingly began to restore it to its former glory. It was somewhat disconcerting to be able to look down and see the road clearly through the gaping holes in the floor. However, after a bit of wizardry with some fibreglass it was as good as new. The brakes, electrics and mechanics were thoroughly checked and reconditioned where necessary. Inside there was a bench seat with a deep shelf above and behind it. These were upholstered with a soft, dark blue fabric and we bought a smart, navy-blue leather cover for the steering-wheel. Finally, the outside bodywork was restored and given a finish of pale blue Hammerite paint.

The Isetta's design was somewhat unusual in that the steering-wheel was attached to the only way in and out of the car - namely the front door. There being no side doors, the whole of the front, which included the windscreen, opened outwards. Thus every time the door was opened, the steering-wheel disappeared with it. It was a prudent driver who made sure the door was securely closed before setting off. The large, curved windscreen, plus two side windows and the rear window, provided excellent all-round vision. The other nice feature was a little sunshine roof which could be slid open in fine weather, yet be firmly closed to keep the occupants snug and dry in wet weather.

The car had three forward gears, a reverse gear and four wheels, the front two being set much wider apart than the rear two. Its manoeuvrability was remarkable. It could turn on the proverbial sixpence and parking it was a dream - just as long as you remembered not to drive right up to a wall or other obstacle. If you did, someone else in a hurry was likely to nip opportunely into the ample space left behind you before you had a chance to gather your belongings together. This happened to me a couple of times, and with no room to open the front door, I had to make an undignified exit through the roof.

A small round object with wheels

I have to admit that I grew very attached to this rotund little vehicle. The children, of course, adored it. They would never go in the 'real' car if there was an option to ride in the Isetta. Predictably, the aircrew were merciless in their leg-pulling. One morning I came out to find a large clockwork key had been fixed to the back. A few days later a notice, purloined from an aircraft, was attached to the rear window. It read *Safe to use at 35,000 feet.* Often I'd come out and not be able to find it at all, the pranksters having manhandled it into some ridiculous, or seriously embarrassing, situation.

The little car served me well throughout my time at Bishop Grosseteste, and I became resigned to people making fun of it. One lovely autumn day I set off for college wearing a track suit in anticipation of a day on the sports field. With a long scarf wound round my neck, it was warm enough to drive with the sunshine roof open. I came to the traffic lights at the foot of a steep hill and pulled into the outside lane beside a big lorry that was waiting for the green light. Looking out of my side window I couldn't see much of the huge vehicle above its front mudguard, but I had a strange feeling I was being watched. I glanced up through the sun-roof to see the driver was leaning out of his open window and staring down at me - a broad grin on his face. I braced myself for the inevitable insult that was sure to follow.

"G'morning, love," he said in a cheerful cockney accent.

"Good morning," I replied politely, feeling somewhat at a disadvantage and not wishing to pursue the conversation.

"Psst, psst."

I looked up again.

"I say, Miss, the stick's fell off your dodgem."

* * * * *

I loved being at college. Although we were obliged to attend lectures and pass exams in academic subjects, the PE department was somewhat set apart from the rest of the students. There were only eighteen of us, and we paired off for course work according to height and whether or not we liked the look of each other. Thereafter we tended to stick with the same partner. Mine was a tall athletic girl with red hair and green eyes, and we became firm friends. She was extremely beautiful, a point not lost on the single fliers, who took to hanging around our house at weekends in the hope she might be coming to stay with us.

The months flew by as they tried to turn us into teachers. Then, suddenly, we were informed that we were about to be let loose on the unsuspecting school-children of the region. It was time for our first teaching practice. Feeling totally inadequate, we were farmed out to various locations in the county. Some went to big comprehensive schools, where the senior pupils were not much younger than the terrified students. I had opted to teach middle school age, and bright and early one Monday morning, I found myself bowling across country, bound for a small village nestling in the Lincolnshire wolds.

I had no idea what to expect as I trundled the Isetta down the hill towards the small, formerly Church of England, school. I had to brake sharply as a horde of children rushed out of the gate and along the road to meet me. No doubt they had never seen anything quite like my car, but still, their reaction was a bit over the top. I might as well have landed in a space ship for all the commotion it caused. They didn't look a bad lot and I relaxed. I had a feeling this might just be a piece of cake compared with the urban nightmares some of my colleagues had drawn. This euphoria lasted right up until I met the headmaster.

He was, you might say, of the old school. Very old. He was also something of a hoarder. Piled up all around the walls of the big classroom were crumpled cardboard boxes and buff-coloured files. They contained the schoolwork of former pupils, dating back to the early 1930s. Covered in dust, they harboured something even worse, as I was to discover later that day.

The children who had rushed out so exuberantly to surround the Isetta now sat quietly at simple wooden desks arranged in straight rows. Facing them was the teacher's desk, raised up on a small platform. Close at hand a large blackboard rested on an easel. A weighty, leather-bound tome lay on the elevated desk, alongside a couple of pieces of chalk and a chalkboard eraser. No other teaching aids were in evidence.

The headmaster quickly made it clear that he didn't much approve of having student teachers foisted upon him. He did not like to have his daily routine upset. I was motioned to a chair beside and below him and the day began, as did every other school day, with a bible reading. The children sat in silence while he thundered fire and brimstone at them for an interminable thirty minutes.

Eventually he closed the enormous book and grudgingly introduced me to the class. There were about twenty pupils of mixed age and ability, including two or three who had severe learning difficulties. They looked at me expectantly. So did he. What did I intend to do with them? I thought of the carefully planned lesson in my briefcase and waffled something about reading to them from The Hobbit and linking it to some artwork. He sniffed at this obviously ridiculous suggestion and said "Well, make sure you remind them to bring their towels and costumes after dinner, it's swimming today."

My spirits immediately lifted. Here I was on familiar ground. Fully qualified in the teaching of swimming, I had previously been employed by several schools as their resident swimming instructor. I cheerfully passed this information on to him, certain that it would gain me a few Brownie points and raise me a notch or two in his estimation. My optimism lasted but a few brief seconds. He was not at all impressed. In fact, he informed me that I would not be accompanying the children to the baths. I was only a student and he could not possibly entrust their safety to the likes of me. They would be in the care of the proper teacher, Mrs Somebody-or-other, who took them every week.

The appointed time came and I met the proper teacher. She was a pleasant elderly lady with a worried expression. She welcomed me to the school, saying she dreaded Monday afternoons.

"I do so hate the water, dear," she said. "I can't swim a stroke."

* * * * *

The bus went off with the swimming party, the headmaster went I know not where, and I was left alone in the school with a pile of exercise books - tasked with familiarising myself with the children's current classwork. It was uncannily quiet. Rays of sunlight penetrated the rather small windows, set high on one wall, and highlighted the thick dust that had accumulated on the boxes and files stored around the room. I lifted my head from my reading a couple of times, thinking I heard a rustling sound. Then once or twice, out of the corner of my eye, I thought I saw something move at the far end of the room. More minutes passed. Then, looking up, I realised I was not seeing and hearing things that didn't exist. Several small brown mice began to emerge from behind the piled-up boxes. They ran hither and thither, scurrying across the floor and climbing up on to the chairs and desks at will. There were dozens of them. I hurled the chalkboard eraser and they vanished like magic, only to reappear a few seconds later.

No one having returned when my allotted time span for the day came, I closed the door quietly on my class of rodents and drove home along the leafy Lincolnshire lanes, with the sunshine roof open to let in the glorious fresh air.

Although I did not realise it, they were taking bets back at college to see how long I would last at the school. So far, no one student had yet stuck the whole course! The mice usually got them on the first day, but if, like me, they didn't freak out at the furry little blighters running amok in the classroom, the bible-thumping head's scathing attitude soon reduced most of them to tears. As it happened, I *did* stick it out. The children loved it on the days I went, and we had a lot of fun setting up an aquarium, then catching tadpoles and sticklebacks to put in it. All pupils participated. They wrote about the project, and those who couldn't drew colourful pictures in illustration. The boy with the greatest learning difficulties delighted in being in charge of the feeding and cleaning programme. The headmaster sniffed. He thought they had plenty of time outdoors as it was. He had them working in the garden for half an hour every day himself. It was the one place in the whole school that was immaculate - well dug over and planted with neat rows of vegetables. There was a fish pond beside the flagged path, and whenever he stamped his foot on one of the loose flagstones, a huge goldfish immediately shoved a gaping mouth above the water to be fed. He was immensely proud of his goldfish trick.

When the time came for me to go back into college, I left the aquarium for the children to enjoy until the end of the school term. I promised to return on the very last day, to say goodbye and to go with them to take the tadpoles, frogs and fish to the stream.

On the appointed day I drove down the hill towards the school with several small gifts for the children and some large glass jars for transporting the aquarium's inmates. The children rushed out to greet me, but they were not laughing as usual. Indeed some of them were crying. It seems that the day I finished my teaching practice, the headmaster fed the tadpoles, one by one, to his monstrous goldfish. Students from the college were not sent to this school again, and within a year or so, on the headmaster's retirement, the Victorian relic closed for ever.

2. CYPRUS HERE WE COME

The time of our departure for sunnier climes drew ever nearer, and the sound of hammering and banging echoed from our garage as Harry nailed up the big wooden boxes that would take our belongings overseas. We went on a wild spending spree in Lincoln, buying summer clothes and new swimsuits. Shop assistants regarded us with envy. Lucky devils! Fancy getting paid to go and live on a Mediterranean island. There followed the usual round of farewell parties, and almost before we knew it, we were on a train heading towards Devon and home. We sped through the familiar, beloved West Country landscape, revelling in the gentle, rolling hills after the flat Lincolnshire terrain. Cows grazing in fields beside the railway track turned their heads to watch us pass. Broad-backed Devon Reds, with their thickly curling coats, and black and white Friesians standing knee-deep in lush grass. I relished the thought of the treat that awaited us later that day. My mother would have junket, sprinkled with nutmeg, and a big bowl of Devonshire clotted cream on the table for tea.

The train steamed into St David's station in Harry's home town of Exeter. I watched a mixture of emotions cross his face as memories began to flood into his mind. Both his parents were dead and he no longer had a family home in the city, but this was where he had grown up and gone to school, sung in the Cathedral, played rugby and cricket, and joined a brass band. Here, too, we had met for the first time.

The whistle blew, the guard waved his green flag, and the train began to pick up speed again. The railway line followed the course of the river Exe for a while, and then we were chugging along beside the mouth of the estuary towards Starcross. Herons waded in the shallow mudflats and stately swans swam down to meet the flood tide. I looked across to the sunlit rooftops of Exmouth on the other shore. My father, a police officer, had been posted there twice, once as an Inspector when I was still at school, and later, on promotion, when I was in my early twenties. We lived in many places within the county of Devon as he was moved around, but I considered Exmouth, above all others, to be my home town.

Dawlish Warren, Dawlish, Teignmouth. We passed through seaside holiday resorts in the region that had been so much a part of our growing up. It was years since we had travelled by train, and the memories conjured up by the journey threatened to overwhelm us at times. Here my brother and I had fished and explored the estuary in our tiny wooden boat. We'd rowed across to the golden sands of Dawlish Warren, where hundreds of wild rabbits lived among the marram grass. Not yet claimed as a prime site for tourism and all the gaudy trappings that accompany it, the lovely, lonely dunes had provided shelter for many species of water bird. Unpolluted water lapped the sandy beach and we dived and swam in its cool green depths.

The train rolled on through territory containing many of the country pubs we had frequented as young adults. Here the brave drank *scrumpy* - rough Devonshire cider brewed from apples in large wooden barrels. That sorted the men from the tourists, who tended to think the locals were rather quaint. A big swallow of the aromatic amber liquid was like drinking old razor blades, and the floor seemed a bit uneven when you went to stand up. The regulars sat on bar stools gleefully watching the uninitiated come to grief. They cheered them on with bawdy songs, usually accompanied by an expert on the spoons. One ancient, in the Seven Stars at Starcross, used to play the bones. Not surprising, one of his supporters had said sagely, for his house was right next door to the cemetery.

All too soon, it seemed, we were slowing down and bowling along beside another estuary as we pulled into Plymouth and headed for the family home. Our last days in England flew swiftly by in a flurry of visits to relatives and nostalgic trips to old haunts. We rode the ferry up river to Calstock, to feast on traditional English fish and chips. We took a boat from Plymouth Hoe across to Cawsand with its narrow streets and white-painted fishermen's cottages. And we climbed to the top of the lighthouse on the Hoe to look out over Plymouth Sound, where Drake had seen the Spanish

Armada approaching. Finally, on a cool English summer day with a fine drizzle falling, we bade our last farewells and headed for Brize Norton, where a Britannia waited to take us to the island that would become our home for the next three years.

* * * * *

The aircraft touched down at RAF Akrotiri early in the morning, and we stepped out into brilliant sunshine. It was August and the heat hit us like a solid wall. It reflected up off the tarmac and grabbed us in its humid grip. The familiar outline of a Vulcan bomber stood nearby on a dispersal pan. It looked strangely alien dressed in its desert camouflage. A pair of Lightning fighters roared down the runway and swept, almost vertically, skyward. The noise was deafening. The ground trembled and the heat haze shimmered intensely. Thankfully, we were not kept hanging about for long, and soon passed into the air-conditioned comfort of the terminal building. Once the formalities had been completed and we passed through customs, we were immediately swept up by friends and colleagues who were waiting to greet us. Then we were heading towards Limassol and the hotel where we would stay that night. Showered and changed into cooler clothing, we began the serious business of the day. We contacted one of the many local property agents, and piling into his car, then began a gruelling and hot tour of the town to find a suitable place to live.

The British Bases were very large in those days and could not accommodate all the married personnel who were posted in, so most of us lived in hirings in Limassol. Many of the houses were beautiful - several seeming to us like something out of a Hollywood film set - but we had to keep within the budget set out by the Royal Air Force for Harry's rank. We had been pre-warned about some of the things to look out for. One colleague had rented a very nice house with a big garage. He moved in, and as was the custom for pretty well all of us, spent the second day choosing the car he would buy to get him to and from his place of work. Once the new duty-free car had been ordered, the car salesman handed over the keys of a *gizzit* which the buyer had free use of until his new car was delivered. This odd name was compiled from the answer given by someone when asked from whence this car came: "He give us it." Like *gazome,* for going-home parties at the end of each tour, the name stuck and is still in use to this day.

The unsuspecting officer and his wife proudly drove the *gizzit* back to their new home. They immediately sensed something was amiss when they noticed the garage door was open. Inside they could see a table, some chairs, a bed and a few other household items. It appears they had rented the house but not the garage. The couple who owned the house had moved in there, in order to be able to collect the generous rent dished out by the Bases for their property. Others found sheds, or old buildings, in their gardens occupied by the family grandmother. Many who moved into flats discovered, too late, that the owners lived directly above or below them and were unable to adjust to the Cypriots' inherent hospitality and tendency to treat them as part of the family. One poor chap opened his woodshed on day two to find a goat in there.

Forewarned is forearmed, and by the following day, we were installed in our very own goat and grandma-free hiring and happily driving our *gizzit* towards the older part of town, determined to explore every inch of it.

* * * * *

A quarter of a century ago, Limassol did not show to the world the face it shows today. There were no supermarkets, at least none appreciably larger than the little old corner shops in provincial England. Fresh produce did not come plastic-wrapped in polystyrene trays. If you wanted fruit and vegetables you went to the market.

Here there was noise and bustle and colour, laughter, arguments and people shouting the praises of their wares. The crowded stalls were banked high with the most magnificent arrays of fresh fruit. Nothing was imported - one ate what was in season, and there was always plenty to choose from. Winter oranges, mandarins, clementines, lemons, grapefruit, apples and pears, were followed by cherries, apricots, peaches and plums in spring and summer. Then it was time for the grapes to be harvested, and how the children loved the tiny green-skinned bananas that were grown at Kouklia. A diversity of green met the eye where the tiered stalls held lettuce, cabbages, spinach, celery, small cucumbers, coriander and flat-leaved parsley. There were onions, spring onions, aubergines, courgettes, marrows, pumpkins and also vegetables we were not familiar with but couldn't wait to try. Ripe red tomatoes glowed alongside smooth-skinned potatoes that were among the best in the world.

Men in bloodstained once-white overalls ran in to the market with huge sides of beef, lamb and pork on their shoulders. The dozen or so butchers in the market hall then smashed it into shapeless, bone-splintered chunks, bellowing its impeccable pedigree as they worked. They hacked away in a frenzy of enthusiasm while ash from their cigarettes dropped on to the wooden chopping blocks and large black flies buzzed incessantly around them. Purchasing meat in those days was not for the faint-hearted or squeamish.

Adjacent to the main hall was the fish market, where huge swordfish lay on marble slabs next to boxes of squid, octopus and many other piscine species we could not identify. In the same hall were long stone counters, where people from outlying villages could hire a pitch and sell their home-grown produce. This was the place where many a good bargain was to be had at the end of the morning.

On one side of the fish stalls a door led through to the poultry market, while on the other, a second doorway led out into the street. Here there were more stalls, and just about everything you could possibly think of was for sale. There were live rabbits, hens, pigeons and day-old chicks; sacks of rice, nuts, grains and dried pulses; boxes of dried fish, baskets of fresh brown eggs, *lounza, loukanika* and a variety of local cheeses. Colourful bales of material were unrolled for housewives to admire and swollen feet were crammed into locally-made leather shoes. Greek music played loudly as the voluble but good-tempered crowd shoved and pushed their way around.

Once you managed to fight your way through here, you came upon the parking place, where buses from all the surrounding villages waited while people completed their business in the big town. Individually painted and gaily coloured, these vehicles were an unusual and picturesque sight. Their drivers lovingly polished imaginary finger marks off the gleaming paintwork and buffed up the silvery mascots of flying swans or tigers fixed on the bonnet as they waited for their passengers to return.

The aromatic smell of freshly-ground coffee enticed us around to the main market square. A few tables were set out, and seated at one were two priests, dressed in long blue robes and stove-pipe hats. They interrupted their conversation to greet us politely. In

Seated at one were two priests

one corner of the square a large Turk sat smoking a *nargileh.* He was sitting on a wooden chair which had a seat of woven straw. His outstretched leg rested on another and his left arm lay across the back of a third. His right hand clutched the red *markouji,* the flexible tube, which led down into the hookah water pipe resting on the floor. The children were fascinated. They stared, hypnotised, at the water bubbling gently beneath the glowing charcoal as he breathed in and out. The smoker ignored them. Eyes heavy-lidded, half-closed, he sat there impassively in a distant world of his own.

Tired, hot, elated and well-stocked with fresh fruit, salad, local cheeses and a round loaf of crusty bread, we made our way home for lunch, to be followed by the almost mandatory siesta. In the hottest summer months everything came to a stop at one o'clock and didn't start up again until four. Houses were shuttered against the sun, ceiling fans were turned on, and everyone slept through the unbearable heat. There were few cars, no massive lorries and no ton-up motorbikes to disturb the slumbering town. Shops reopened in the late afternoon, and in the cool of the evening, Limassolians promenaded along the narrow seafront road and dined with friends in the open-air tavernas.

That evening we had plans to explore St. Andrew's Street and the old Turkish Quarter before meeting up with friends to try, for the first time, the renowned Doner kebab. St. Andrew's St was narrow, crowded, and teeming with life and colour. Darkroomed bazaars, with rickety wooden staircases and precarious ladders to descend down into the basement areas, were full to bursting with sheepskins from which coats could be made to measure. There were huge piles of soft leather for jackets, shoes and handbags which could be hand-fashioned to your choice - ready almost before the ink was dry on the scraps of paper used for order forms. There were sheepskin rugs from Turkey and pony-skin rugs from Iran. There were camel stools from Egypt, Persian carpets, beaten copper from Syria, and hand-carved woodwork. Exquisite boxes and backgammon sets in polished marquetry were displayed alongside jewellery from the Lebanon and delicate blue glassware from Hebron. It was like being let loose in Aladdin's cave.

We walked along the street, which was the veritable heart of the old town, stepping around bolts of cloth that spilled out on to the pavement and ducking under tablecloths and crochet-work hanging above us. At the far end of the road, we came upon an old mosque, an ancient bath-house which had a rounded dome inset with green bottles, and another market place. We had entered the Turkish Quarter.

Here were metal-workers by the dozen, the murky interiors of their shops stacked with galvanised buckets and the narrow doorways festooned with pots and pans. Numerous other small workshops professed to repair anything and everything under the sun. There were watchmakers, coppersmiths and silversmiths. One establishment made Turkish Delight, and the proprietor beckoned us inside to taste the gelatinous sweetmeat and see how it was packaged and labelled. At one end of the Turkish territory was the tall minaret of the community's mosque, and nearby a park where coloured lights were strung across between the trees. In this cool and shady place, women in flowing dresses and colourful headscarves sat gossiping while children laughed and played around them.

We slowly retraced our steps, looking out for a large white building set back from the road. A red crescent would indicate that it was the Turkish hospital, and it was here that we had arranged to meet our friends.

Evening was drawing on by the time we spotted them sitting on a low wall outside the hospital. By then we were all feeling hungry again, but our hosts assured us that would not remain the case for long. They indicated a shabby-looking shop window across the road. It didn't look like much of a restaurant from the outside, and even less so once you entered. There were only three or four wooden tables spread with dingy oilcloths, and a dozen or so chairs. A bell over the door clanged as we went in, and the Doner kebab man came to greet us warmly. He pushed two of the tables together to accommodate all of us and we sat down. He disappeared through a bead curtain into another room and a sudden and delicious aroma assailed our nostrils. He was soon back with plates and cutlery, salad, yoghurt and some warm *chapattis.* He then invited us into the kitchen to

We came upon an old mosque

see our meal cooking. I had never seen a Doner kebab before. It was a huge, carrot-shaped piece of beef rotating vertically in front of a gas-powered grill, so that the meat cooked from the outside. As it browned, he expertly carved thin slices downwards and laid them on our plates. The tender, juicy meat was sprinkled with spices before it was served and there was as much as you could eat for the all-in ridiculous price of four shillings - complete with as much *kokinelli* as you could drink. It was delicious. We made firm friends with the owner, and the place became one of our favourite venues during the early seventies.

We drove home, feeling that life was treating us pretty well. The children, exhausted by all the excitement, were asleep almost as soon as they fell into bed, but we were to sit for some time in the garden beneath a canopy of fragrant jasmine, enjoying the balmy night air and reliving the events of the past few days.

3. KYRENIA

The following weeks saw us settling into our new life. Schools were closed for the summer holiday, and while Harry worked long hours getting used to his new job, the children and I took time to explore our surroundings. In 1971 Episkopi was a large base housing RAF Headquarters Near East Command, and with so many families living in Limassol, it was easy for working colleagues to double up in cars travelling to work, thus leaving some available for wives left at home. The main working day began at the relatively cool hour of seven o'clock and continued until one-thirty when, hot and perspiring, hundreds of servicemen drove, nose to tail, back into town in the midday heat.

At four o'clock, when the sun's trajectory was lower in the sky, we headed for the beach. The ideal place for swimming was at Ladies' Mile with its endless length of golden sand. The sea was clear and shallow, and the children soon became bronzed as they frolicked in the warm water and played on the beach with their friends. Sometimes we swam near the Municipal Gardens in Limassol, where a long wooden pier jutted out into the sea. Here we dangled our legs or floated lazily on air beds while our offspring spent many happy hours climbing over and diving from the sturdy old construction. A lack of hotels and apartment blocks meant that bathers had easy access to the beach all the way along the seafront. The sand was greyish and rather gritty, but the swimming was good and the area was shaded from the road by trees and shrubs.

At weekends we ventured further afield, discovering a deserted place that was marvellous for swimming, called Governor's Beach. Not too far away was the tiny seaside village of Zygi, which had been a flashpoint of trouble between Greek and Turkish Cypriots in the past. All was quiet on the surface, though, and we wandered around its few houses warmly greeted by both communities. We drank thick sweet Turkish coffee with families of obvious Moorish descent and ate fresh fish just taken from the sea by Greek fishermen. We could not foresee then that such a tragic end would befall many of them in 1974.

* * * * *

Once we were well and truly settled in and had taken possession of our new car, my erstwhile college friend, Josie, whose husband was now serving with 35 Squadron at Akrotiri, telephoned to say that two or three families from the squadron were going to Kyrenia for the weekend. Would we care to join them? Would we? We couldn't wait to explore more of this fascinating and beautiful place.

Saturday dawned and we set off early in three cars. There were six of us accompanied by seven children of a roughly similar age. On the outskirts of Nicosia we passed a United Nations position with white-painted DUKW vehicles parked in a neat row outside. Not far away a red flag with the sickle moon and star of Turkey fluttered above an army camp. We progressed without difficulty, however, and soon had our first clear sight of Pentadactylos, the five-fingered mountain that punched the sky like a giant fist. It was an impressive sight, and one I have never forgotten. Shortly after this came the first indication, to us on a personal level, that all was not well in this island paradise. A line of cars, with the occupants sitting inside, had pulled up at the side of the road. A UN vehicle was positioned at the head of the column. We slowed as we passed by, and shortly afterwards we were stopped by armed Turkish soldiers. Once they had scrutinised our navy-blue British passports, they waved us on without comment. We swept on down into the lovely little harbour town of Kyrenia, and there, as we sat downing some welcome cold drinks, I learned that the cars contained perfectly law-abiding Greek Cypriot citizens. We, as strangers, were allowed to pass freely by, but they had to wait for a UN convoy to escort them through at ten o'clock in the morning. The convoy would then reform at four o'clock for those who wished to make the return journey that day. I felt uncomfortable and ill at ease to bear witness to this unhappy situation.

There was time to visit Bellapais before lunch, and we set off up the narrow winding road that led to the village. The cars ground slowly upward in low gear until we reached the square, which is dominated by the ruin of the lovely abbey. Its mellow stones glowed in the clear light, and the late-morning sunshine cast deep shadows beneath graceful arches. Slender green cypress trees pointed beseechingly heavenwards as though in supplication to an unseen God. We gazed towards Kyrenia, lying far below us, and caught our breath at the wonder of it. This, surely, must be one of the most beautiful views in the world. The verdant, tree-clad land sloped steeply down towards the coast, the colours softening and merging in the shimmering heat-haze. The sea sparkled with the blue intensity of a flawless sapphire, its panoramic vastness diffusing into a distant, misty horizon.

It was quiet in the square. Behind me I could hear the click-clack of backgammon and the soft murmur of Greek voices. A few old men were sitting in the shade beneath the Tree of Idleness. Two were occupied with their game of backgammon, while a third, leaning forward and resting his hands on an intricately-carved walking stick, offered advice to each player in turn. Others simply sat back in their chairs, heads nodding, drowsy in the noon-day heat.

At the coffee shop they asked us whether we wanted to visit Buffavento. This wind-buffeted castle was perched high on a mountain top and was not easily

There was time to visit Bellapais

accessible by car, certainly not by someone with no head for heights. From Bellapais, however, you could travel by donkey along a six or seven mile track. Moreover, your guide would provide refreshment, and the trip could be made in leisurely fashion. The children were all in favour of leaping on the donkeys there and then, but we realised it called for a whole day to be set aside, plus a bit of preparation beforehand - not to mention finding something to rub into saddle-sore limbs afterwards. We vowed to make this particular journey on our next visit to Kyrenia.

We rolled down the steep hill once more, to lunch at the police canteen in a side-street by the castle. Here we were given the warmest of welcomes by policemen and customs officers eating their midday meal. We joined them for the most delicious local food we had tasted so far, and then it was time to relax and swim for a while. The children couldn't wait to get into the water. Clambering into the cars again, we headed along the coast towards Snake Island Beach. I never did see any snakes there, but it was a marvellous place to swim. Undeveloped and in its natural state, it became a favourite haunt of ours whenever we visited the northern part of the island. The children were in their element, inventing elaborate Robinson Crusoe games and swimming and diving in the crystal-clear water.

We stayed overnight at the Dome, Kyrenia's best-known hotel, and the following day explored the castle. It was still early as we drove along the lovely

The precipitous heights of St Hilarion

coastline to the monastery of Lambousa - built in isolation on the rocky shoreline. From here it was a short drive to the green and shady village of Lapithos to visit the renowned potteries.

We enjoyed a leisurely lunch and a swim, before setting off to find the second of the three fairytale castles in the northern range. After pursuing a steep, contorted track which hugged the side of a mountain, we eventually left the vehicles well below the summit, and climbed the last back-breaking metres to the precipitous heights of St Hilarion. It was as if we had stepped out of the world and now viewed it from another place. There was an uninterrupted view - to infinity, it seemed. To look down made me feel slightly giddy and I marvelled at the imagination and daring of those who had built here. I passed through a doorway and, looking landward, caught my breath and steadied myself against the stone wall. Just below me, in silent, gliding flight, an Imperial eagle swept past. I could clearly see the plumage, the cruelly-hooked beak and the brilliant eye of the massive bird. It was a magical moment in time, and I felt my heart would stop. To me this glorious creature symbolised power and freedom and awe-inspiring beauty.

We returned to Limassol later that day, full of the wonders we had seen and feeling an ever-increasing affinity for the island and its warm, hospitable people. Already, the three-year tour we had been allocated seemed too short. Time was flying by.

* * * * *

We had been anticipating a move into married quarters at Episkopi as soon as one became available. Suddenly, however, the situation changed. Harry was tasked with setting up an adult education centre in Limassol. This was so that all British Forces personnel and their dependants living there could avail themselves of the same facilities for evening classes that were offered by local authorities in the UK. A suitable building was provided on the By-Pass. This had been constructed to ease congestion in the narrow streets of the main town. It was, predictably, named Archbishop Makarios III Avenue, and the sides of the road were planted with lovely trees which were laden with pink and white blossom in early spring. To no one's surprise, it became more and more of a built-up area, lined with shops and offices. It was a standing joke that sooner or later a by-pass would have to be constructed to by-pass the By-Pass.

Part-time teachers were recruited, and before long, you could take O and A levels in practically anything. Subjects like shorthand and typing, dressmaking, art and flower-arranging quickly became popular, and the centre was always a hive of industry.

There was now no point in our going to live at Episkopi, where Harry would have to travel all the way back to Limassol to work each day, so we were offered a quarter at Berengaria on the outskirts of Polemidia.

The children were already attending school there, travelling the mile or so each day by bus. Now it would be a two-minute walk for them, and Harry would have only a very short journey to work. Out came the boxes again, and a couple of weeks later we were unpacking our belongings once more into yet another home.

Berengaria was a British enclave where the houses were rather like pre-fabs. They were all bungalows - spacious, airy, and set in gardens planted with lovely flowering shrubs and trees. Ours was formerly the Colonel's residence. It looked like the nine-fifteen to Paddington, having a long corridor, with corresponding outside verandah, running the entire length of the building. Four bedrooms, three bathrooms and a study were accessed from this, while a door at the end led into a large living-room, which had French windows opening on to the garden. Finally came the kitchen and a utility room. It was perfect.

Our very large garden was well cared-for. Geraniums and oleander flowered brightly alongside blood-red hibiscus and starry, night-scented jasmine. Apricot-coloured bougainvillaea sprawled up and over one end of the roof, and welcome shade was provided by a variety of trees. Lining the front of the garden was a row of poinsettia trees which had grown tall and sturdy over the years. We'd have a magnificent display of scarlet bracts when Christmas came. Between the kitchen and the wide driveway to the garage was a huge mature fig tree. The back garden was bounded by a long dry-stone wall overlooking fields and open spaces towards the Troodos mountains. A single small hill rose up a few hundred metres away, its shape giving rise to its English name of Beehive Hill.

Berengaria had been built close to the villages of Pano and Kato Polemidia, and both Greek and Turkish Cypriots found employment within the British enclave. Thus, when we took possession of our new home, we found we had inherited a Turkish batwoman. Safia was a small, work-worn woman, grown old before her time. She had five children and an out-of-work husband to support. She desperately needed the job, and I simply didn't have the heart to tell her that, never having had the luxury of a batwoman before, we did not really require her services. To tell the truth, though, once we became accustomed to having her around, I don't know how we would have managed without her. She kept the huge place in spotless condition, and whenever we attended a Mess function, she was eager to baby-sit to earn a little more. She did not speak English, but spoke Greek fluently. I was already making inroads into this difficult language, so we communicated mainly in Greek while passing on to each other a smattering of English and Turkish.

She was worth every *piastre.* As well as being industrious and efficient, she was clean, polite, honest and truly fond of the children. Harry needed a freshly washed and ironed khaki drill uniform each day and Safia revelled in providing this service. That alone made her indispensable as far as I was concerned. Full of pleated pockets and creases that must be sharp and crisp, KDs were a nightmare for someone like me, who can't iron a handkerchief without first folding it in four to lessen the task.

Safia invited me to her home in the village one day. She was at the door to greet me, and I stepped into the tiny house, shocked at the extreme poverty in which she lived. The earthen floors were swept clean and the faded cloth which covered the few dilapidated chairs had been washed and ironed. On the one small, low table a jam-jar full of wild flowers rested on a crocheted mat. There was an old wooden dresser, which had a glass-fronted cupboard containing some oddments of china and a water jug. Children's shoes, mostly in need of repair, were arranged neatly in pairs beneath the dresser. A plastic-strip curtain covered a doorway leading, presumably, to a kitchen; for the eldest daughter, who was about twelve years old, came through bearing a tin tray with several glasses of orange squash. Behind her was a younger child carrying a plate of biscuits.

I sat on one of the chairs and Safia, obviously delighted to be acting as hostess, settled opposite me. The eldest daughter was despatched to make thick sweet Turkish coffee, and one by one, the other children came in to greet me politely. There were three girls and two boys. The youngest girl, smiling shyly, cradled a crudely-carved wooden doll. Their clothing was shabby, but clean. Their black hair shone with cleanliness and health

- the girls having theirs braided into thick plaits. They were bright happy souls, and Safia was patently proud of both her offspring and her tiny home.

When I took my leave, Safia walked with me to the end of the street where I had left the car. She indicated a group of men sitting, smoking their inevitable cigarettes, at a coffee shop on the corner. One was her husband. He rose as he saw her pointing him out and came across to shake hands. He was swarthy, rather slightly built, and, not unexpectedly, appeared dispirited. He greeted me with civility in Turkish, but I noticed that his polite smile did not quite reach his eyes.

I was sobered by this visit. When I arrived home, our well-furnished and equipped married quarter appeared positively opulent in comparison. I had so much, while because of a situation beyond her control, Safia had so little.

Over dinner that evening I described the circumstances in which our batwoman lived, and mentioned how well looked-after the children were, despite their lack of material things. Later, when I went to kiss my own children goodnight, a lump came into my throat. For, of their own volition, Karen, ten years old and Jeremy, just seven, had set aside several of their favourite toys to give to Safia's children. I looked at their soap-shiny, eager little faces as they earnestly discussed with each other the suitability of what they had chosen. I found it strangely difficult to speak, but I had never felt more proud of them in my life.

4. SNOWFALL ON TROODOS

That winter there was very heavy snowfall on the Troodos mountains, and with some leave outstanding, several of us decided to go up to the Services Leave Centre for a few days. There was excellent skiing and anything one needed could be borrowed from the stores. Once kitted out, skiers were ferried up to the mountain in a big army lorry.

There was a Cyprus ski-club, but Cypriots who indulged in winter sports were relatively few. The slopes were mainly used by British Forces and United Nations personnel. There was a large Austrian UN contingent stationed on the island, and among them were some expert ski instructors. Harry was already accomplished in the art, having trained in Canada and also spent time skiing in Scotland, while I had never had a go. To be candid, by the time I had picked myself up for the umpteenth time, I didn't feel I'd been terribly deprived. Our daughter took to it immediately, but our small son, deciding sledging looked a lot more fun, hurled himself down the adjoining slope on a big steel-runnered sledge.

"That thing is a bit fast," said Harry. "You'd better go down with him and make sure he misses the trees." Oh well, I was spending most of my time sitting

Snowfall on Troodos

down anyway.

"Great, Mum," said Jeremy. "It'll go a lot faster with two of us."

He was right - it did. And it was a whole lot more fun than skiing!

Tired, but exhilarated, after a few hours of whizzing down the snow-covered mountain we made our way to Smokey Joe's to thaw ourselves out and sip big mugs of hot chocolate. Smokey Joe's was a small ramshackle cabin where everyone crowded in to warm up by a wood-burning stove and swap stories of personal prowess and the day's hair-raising escapes. Here you could catch up on the news and leave messages for your friends. Run by a larger-than-life local character, no skiing trip was complete without a visit to Smokey Joe's.

The three-tonner arrived to take us back to the Leave Centre. Hot baths and fresh warm clothing, then, with our friends assembled around a crackling log fire and the children all playing monopoly together, we toasted the day's success in *glühwein,* the traditional after-ski drink.

Having dined, the younger family members were soon in bed - physically exhausted by their energetic day. We stayed by the blazing pine logs, talking and reminiscing for a while, but it was not long before we too began to find it difficult to keep our eyes open.

"Must be the heat from that fire," said Bill, downing his sixth tumbler of the spiced mulled wine.

Several heads nodded sagely in agreement, and somewhat unsteadily we wound our way towards the sleeping quarters.

The following morning we awoke to find a severe blizzard in the night had blanketed the Leave Centre, and drifting snow had buried some of the cars. The children were ecstatic. They had visions of being marooned in the mountains and not having to go to school again until the spring thaw.

The army had snow-ploughs out at first light, clearing the roads. Shovel parties were busy uncovering paths and walkways outside, while the appetising aroma of sizzling bacon drifted from the kitchen. Breakfast all prepared - this was luxury indeed. We set to with a will.

The pistes were not open, so we decided to wrap up well before setting off on foot to explore the surrounding area. We stepped outside to a breathtaking winter scene. The snowstorm had passed and the sky was a cloudless cornflower blue. Frozen snow scrunched under our feet and large icicles hung like stalactites from the eaves of the low buildings. When we spoke, our warm breath vaporised in the frosty air.

We trudged along the road and made our way to the nearest high point. At the top we stopped to regain our breath and look around. It was bitterly cold and utterly beautiful. The mountains were covered in virgin snow, its pristine whiteness glistening in the sun's early rays. A fresh white mantle shrouded the pine trees on the slopes, while the contours of crags and rock escarpments were softened with a thick covering of crystalline purity. Sounds were strangely muffled. It seemed eerily silent, as though the very forest was asleep. Snow-covered mountains rolled mistily away into the distance in a picturesque scene of Alpine winter perfection. Yet far below us at the coast, we knew it would be warmer than an average English summer. Word had it that Cyprus was one of the few places in the world where you could ski in the morning and, a couple of hours later, swim in the sea. Tomorrow, after a final session on the piste, we intended to put this theory to the test.

The next day we were out early on the slopes in perfect skiing conditions. Two hours later we checked with the Met office at Akrotiri on the weather forecast for the coast. It was to be fine and sunny. We decided to start down the mountain as soon as we had changed our clothes and packed up the cars. Our destination was Shark's Cove, a small, sheltered bay not far from some of the married quarters at RAF Akrotiri. Here we would try out the ski and swim on the same day theory and follow it up with a big, early supper.

The snow-ploughs had been working non-stop since dawn and the roads from the summit were open to four-wheel-drive vehicles and cars with snow-chains. We set off with care. As we descended, however, conditions rapidly improved and we were soon able to discard both the chains and the extra layers of clothing. It was like going from winter to spring in a matter of an hour or so. The snow line disappeared and the countryside was clothed in fresh greenery. The branches of the cherry trees at Perapedi were still bare and apples and plums had not yet burst into bud, but sprays of almond blossom were beginning to appear in the valleys, and tall asphodels were blooming in profusion.

At Phassouri the trees in the plantation were laden with golden oranges, lemons and grapefruit. We drove slowly towards Akrotiri through the tunnel of cypress trees bordering the plantation. In the orchards local women, wearing colourful *mandila,* waved from the tops of wooden ladders as they picked the ripe fruit and laid it in wicker baskets.

Then came one of the loveliest sights of Cyprus. On our left the big salt lake, a dry and barren expanse in summer, was flooded - forming an opaque, turquoise-green lagoon. In its shallow nutrient-rich waters, hundreds of pink flamingos stood on red stilt-like legs, their long elegant necks bending down to sieve vegetable matter, worms and small crustaceans from the bottom of the lake. It was a spectacle of unmatchable beauty and colour. The dark green trees of the plantation lay along one side of the mystical lake, and beyond the blue Mediterranean sparkled under a cloudless sky. The massed cloud of pink on the silvery-green water surged and swayed, as the large birds swept the bottom sand with their uniquely-curved bills, and a gregarious goose-like gaggling reached our ears.

A sudden burst of sound exploded over the lake. A bright yellow helicopter from 84 Squadron roared in, banking steeply before hovering to touch down on the airfield. Many of the birds rose up in alarm, their red and black wings lifting them into clumsy honking flight. They circled slowly a few times, then, as all fell quiet, settled again to resume feeding with the rest of the flock.

The sun was warm on our faces as we watched the flamingos, and we were mindful that we could not dally for long. It was time to test that ski-swim theory. Our little convoy passed through the main gate and up on to the cliffs behind the married quarters. It was a fairly steep climb down over a narrow track to get to the cove, but well worth it. Sheltered from the wind, the little bay had a large flat slab of rock with easy access into deep turquoise water with excellent swimming and snorkelling. The children undressed and, shrieking, flung themselves in - each anxious to claim to be first to take part in the experiment. The rest of us, not to be outdone by our offspring, put a brave face on it and dived in. It was cold at first, but exhilarating when you got used to it. I'm ashamed to admit I was the first to clamber out - wondering how I ever survived the years of training in an open-air seawater swimming-pool, the temperature of which averaged about 13 degrees Celsius in the spring. This was positively warm in comparison.

Dried off and warmly dressed in track-suits, we climbed the cliff path again. We were all agreed that the guide books did not lie. You could ski on Troodos and a few hours later you could swim in the sea. We had done it. Now we were glowing, tingling with well-being

Lifting them into clumsy, honking flight

and exceedingly hungry to boot.

Josie, a mastermind of organisation, had taken the precaution of telephoning ahead to her batwoman, requesting that she take two large containers of her famous chicken curry from the freezer to thaw. Now she set us all in action and the kitchen buzzed with activity. We boiled rice, crisped poppadoms and prepared garnishes and salad, while the curry heated slowly on the hob. The children set the table and the men brought in wood and got a fire going in the big open fireplace. This done, they set up the bar and began sampling its delights. Things looked as though they were going to shape up into a memorable evening.

They did. The curry was hot, the wine chilled and the fire warm. We were the only family not living on the base and, as the evening progressed, the thought of the drive back to Limassol, after such an eventful day, did not impress us. The children were all playing happily together upstairs. Josie went up to tell our two they would be staying the night, only to find that her daughters had already dug out sleeping bags and pillows and were discussing who would sleep in a bed and who would be lucky enough to sleep on a mattress on the floor.

Later that night I lay in bed enveloped in a feeling of warm comradeship, and thankful for the many close and lasting friendships we had forged in our itinerant way of life. When I finally closed my eyes, it was to dream of ethereal winged creatures, drifting like clouds of pink candy-floss, in a slow and graceful ballet on a green and silver lake.

* * * * *

Later that month Harry came home with an invitation for me to visit the Station Commander's wife at Episkopi. These social niceties reared their head every now and then, and I dutifully turned up like a lamb to the slaughter, having no idea what was coming. There was a barrage of senior officers' wives in attendance who, between them, were responsible for organising various charitable and fund-raising events and ensuring that things like Thrift Shops and Wives Clubs ran smoothly.

Always prepared to run a stall or bake a cake when asked, I still didn't smell a rat. It was only when they began to discuss the Limassol Wives Club that I felt the first twinge of unease. They remarked how much of a necessity it was, with so many young wives resident off the base. Then they mused on how poorly attended it was. I gave an inward groan. They were going to ask me outright to join. I hated belonging to any kind of club or society. I preferred to be a free agent. There was still so much to explore and so much to learn about this island. I searched frantically inside my head for excuses to forestall their suggestion. Agoraphobia? Allergic reaction to large numbers of women together? Hang on, they met upstairs - so how about vertigo or can't stand heights? It was no use. Everything sounded lame.

I waited for the inevitable. All eyes turned to look at me as the most senior wife present, smiling confidently, spoke.

"As you are the only senior officer's wife from this station currently residing in Limassol, Sheila, we feel it would be appropriate for you to take over the Limassol Wives Club."

I gazed at her in horror. They didn't just want me to join it - they wanted me to *run* it. My former life flashed before my eyes. Up until now I had managed to avoid the various Wives Clubs where we were stationed. I always had a cast-iron alibi, like a teaching commitment or a college course, to back me up. I definitely did my bit helping out on open days and fêtes, though. In my time I had run cake-stalls, bottle-stalls, hoop-la, and welly-throwing. I even once sat on a plastic chair and got dunked in a tub of water every time some idiot threw a ball and hit the right target. This, however, was a disaster. I had no idea how to run a Wives Club. I had no idea what they did at this Wives Club, and I certainly had no wish to do it myself, whatever it was.

My feeble protestations were swiftly brushed aside. I was without the proverbial leg to stand on. I lived in Limassol, my husband worked in Limassol, and my children would be in school (in Limassol of course) at the time of the Wives Club meeting. In any case, I had my Turkish batwoman to rely on if pressure of Wives Club should delay my return home at any given time. It was no good. They had my number, they knew all about me.

Their victim safely hooked, they quickly stood up - anxious to disperse. A folder was pushed into my hands and I was assured that there were one or two extremely knowledgeable wives of NCOs who would assist me with the utmost willingness and competence. I could also call on the services of a certain bus company whenever I organised away trips. Away trips? Where was I supposed to go, and what did I do when I got there? How on earth could I get myself out of this mess?

Driving back to Limassol I tried to think what it might take to free me from this obligation. I couldn't come up with anything other than getting pregnant again, and the thought of that scared me so much that I decided to shut up and get on with the Wives Club. It couldn't be as bad as all that, surely? If only I had known.

5. THANK GOD FOR IBRAHIM

I quickly called a meeting of my generals to review the situation. The club met one morning a week at a central venue on the By-Pass. There were about forty members, not all of whom attended every meeting. It appeared that members got together to drink coffee and have a chat in a large room above a bar. Although many sessions were given over to playing bingo, they sometimes went on a coach-trip to Paphos or Troodos to 'see' the island. Once they went to Nicosia for 'shopping'. It all sounded pretty tame, so I decided I would try to put a bit of spice into their lives.

The following Tuesday I duly turned up to find myself confronted with some thirty-five women. They appeared to have an age span of approximately thirty years - the younger wives being in their early twenties and the older ones in their fifties. I introduced myself and immediately threw myself at their mercy by saying I knew absolutely nothing about running a Wives Club, but with their help I intended to have a go and make Tuesdays something they would look forward to. I then outlined a few of my ideas and asked for their suggestions.

To my utter amazement, they entered into the

situation with great enthusiasm. Hands were raised, likes and dislikes viewed and future projects, some of which were quite bizarre, discussed. It occurred to me that most of these women were seriously bored. They lived in private hirings which were scattered haphazardly around Limassol. Their husbands left for work before six-thirty in the morning and did not return until about two-thirty in the afternoon. With children at school, this left them with hours of free time on their hands. Most had no transport, and unless they had the company of another British wife living nearby, they found the days were lonely and seemingly endless.

I assured them their lives were about to become a little more adventurous - well, on Tuesdays at least. I was making no promises but I could pretty well guarantee they wouldn't be bored. To this end, as the first rather ambitious project for the new-look Wives Club, I intended to commandeer a lorry from the Bases and enter a float in the big Limassol Carnival which was coming up in a few weeks. By the time we met the following Tuesday, we would need to have come up with a theme.

An excited buzz went round the room. I think half of them thought I was kidding and the other half thought I was mad. Nevertheless, it was the sole topic of conversation over the coffee-break and it looked like being a winner as far as the majority of them were concerned.

Next came the almost mandatory game of

bingo. For the uninitiated, it isn't just anyone who can take on the job of calling out the numbers. I had assumed it would be as easy as pie, but not so. You simply cannot refer to numbers just as they are. They all have to be accompanied with things like ducks, fat ladies, legs and so on. The only one I got right was thirteen. Actually, my ignorance in this field turned out to be quite an ice-breaker. They were a good-natured crowd, and there was a lot of laughter and joshing as they tried to put me right. I never could see the lure of the game myself, but in the ensuing weeks and months, I was often to give fervent thanks to the genius who had invented it in the first place.

At the next meeting more than fifty women showed up and they unanimously approved my list of forthcoming events. These included several local visits they themselves had requested, as well as one or two long distance coach trips I had in mind. It was also decided that the entry for the Carnival would have St Trinian's School as its theme. Coffee was served and the ladies settled around the room to await the arrival of my first guest speaker, a florist who ran a successful flower-shop some little way along the By-Pass. She was going to give a demonstration in the art of flower-arranging.

I glanced, somewhat anxiously, at my watch. She was already late, and the bare wooden table was beginning to look more barren by the moment. The club secretary checked the letter to make sure we had the right date. No mistake - there it was, in writing, telling us she would be delighted to come today. She would bring everything she needed, requiring only that we provide a fairly large table. I asked my followers to talk amongst themselves for a moment while I sent a runner down to the shop to find out why there was a delay. She was soon back and I went down to meet her at the door, ready to greet our guest. The messenger, however, was alone and she looked panic-stricken. She spoke without waiting for my query.

"She says she's too busy to come today - she'll come another time."

My heart sank. My first effort was a disaster before it could even get off the ground. I had visions of being lynched by the fifty or so women upstairs, who were waiting expectantly for the entertainment I had promised them. I grabbed a limp-looking daffodil from a bowl on the bar and, holding it before me, I entered the room with an expressionless face.

"About this flower-arranging..."

At this the whole place erupted into laughter. I have no idea why. I can only presume that they were expecting someone with bowls of flowers and bags of equipment and my single pathetic bloom struck them as funny. My life not appearing to be in imminent danger, I stood my ground and told them the truth. I was mightily relieved that they took it in such good part, but I still had a slight problem. What on earth was I going to do for the next couple of hours? There was nothing for it. One of the helpers got out the bingo.

This event set the pattern for the whole of my time at the Wives Club. I was a bit slow to learn that an arrangement in writing, even if it were to be made by the chairman of the company, stamped with the Royal Seal and signed by the Pope, was no guarantee that someone would show up on the appointed day to fulfil the obligation. Something nearly always went wrong with my carefully-arranged programme. It was absolutely uncanny - as though I was being put to the test every week.

So you thought you had it all well-organised? Get yourself out of that one, Sheila.

Even more strange was the fact that the Wives Club members seemed to find it hilarious. They couldn't wait to see what would happen to me next. Word got round, and as the weeks went by, more and more women enrolled. I started with around forty, but by the end of the first term the membership had more than trebled.

I had a Turkish driver at my disposal. He was a big genial man with a wide grin, and he just loved escorting all the British ladies to the away venues. Nothing was too much trouble for Ibrahim, and nothing threw him off-balance. He grew to understand me perfectly. Sometimes there were so many of us that we needed two buses. This never seemed to pose a problem. One phone call and he would show up with another coach and driver.

I very soon became an expert in improvisation. In this I was assisted by Ibrahim, who quickly got the message after the first away-day disaster. This outing actually turned to worms because of the weather. We went to the Phasouri citrus plantation where members would be able to wander in the orchards while the oranges were being picked, then follow them through the sorting, washing, and packing processes to the sheds where they were boxed and labelled ready for export.

We turned up just as the rain came down. The heavens opened and it poured non-stop. It would have made a monsoon look like an April shower. All picking stopped, and as there were no oranges to process, the rest of the place came to a grinding halt as well. The management were sincerely apologetic. Their shrugs of *what can we do?* were genuine.

My mind was a bit of a blank at this point, but hearing several of the women saying they could do with a cup of coffee, I loaded the thirsty ladies up on to the buses again and (thankfully at someone else's suggestion) headed for Kolossi where, apparently, an excellent cup of Nescafé could be obtained. The sun had broken through the cloud cover as the buses pulled up outside Kolossi castle. In its watery rays the mellow stonework looked clean and newly-washed. It was an impressive building in a good state of preservation. Built by the Knights Templar of St John, it stood among vineyards that produced the grapes used in the making of their

Kolossi castle

famous Commanderia wine. Whenever I climbed the spiralling stairs, or explored the rooms with their huge stone fireplaces, I found it easy to imagine the knights and their ladies, in mediaeval dress, going about their daily lives.

Almost opposite the castle was a place which could, with the best of intentions, be termed a shack. It made Smokey Joe's look like the Ritz. The *kafejis* came out almost rubbing his hands in glee. I stepped down and asked if he would be able to provide coffee for all of us.

"No problem," he said.

In those days, I had not been subjected to the various nuances of those oft-repeated words, so we duly disembarked and traipsed inside. I have to admit the chap was obliging, if a bit on the ambitious side. He boiled up some water, found some evaporated milk, and began tearing open little packets of Nescafé. He was fairly quick at serving the first eleven ladies, but then he ran out of cups. I glanced desperately at Ibrahim. He grinned and shrugged his shoulders.

"Ibrahim, you will have to take us somewhere."

He looked at me aghast.

"Where, Mrs Sheila?"

"I don't know. Anywhere. Take us on a grand mystery tour."

His grin returned. We piled into the buses again and off we went. We drove up into the foothills of the Troodos mountains, passing through small, picturesque villages. The rain had slackened off, and by the time we stopped to admire and photograph a shepherd with his flock of sheep and goats, the sun was shining and the sky was clear and blue. Ibrahim disappeared briefly to use the village telephone. When he came back, his grin had broadened.

"OK, Mrs Sheila, coffee arranged for ladies."

He drove down towards Limassol and along the narrow seafront road to the Turkish quarter. Here, tables had been set out for us in the park adjacent to one of the coffee shops. It was warm in the morning sunshine and we were immediately made welcome. Coffee was served, and as we sipped it, the proprietor's wife brought us plates of locally-made Turkish Delight. Best of all, as far as I was concerned, everyone seemed to be enjoying it. Instead of a disaster, they looked on the morning's outing as a bit of an adventure. We didn't even have to resort to bingo.

Thereafter, whenever things went wrong on an away trip, Ibrahim, grinning from ear to ear, would look at me and raise his eyebrows: "Mystery tour, Mrs Sheila?"

From a distance, in England, my mother reckoned my exploits were better than the silent movie series of her youth entitled The Perils of Pauline. Knowing my love of the ridiculous, I'm pretty certain she thought most of it was exaggerated. But she changed her mind when, during one of her regular visits to Cyprus, she came with us on one of our away days.

In the early nineteen seventies tensions continued to run high between the Greek Cypriot and Turkish Cypriot communities. Supporters of EOKA wanted enosis, or union with Greece. There was a growing militancy, and buildings all over the island, including churches, were defaced with the dark blue paint of EOKA-B slogans. Greece was then run by the Greek colonels, who formed a military *junta,* while here in Cyprus the charismatic Archbishop Makarios was head of both church and state. Understandably, the Turks were not in favour of enosis and the United Nations kept an uneasy peace between the two sides.

In our capacity as British Service wives, we were told to be impartial at all times, and not to get involved in the politics of a foreign country. However, we were free to come and go in all areas at will. Thus, on this particular day, Ibrahim and his second-in-command drove us along the narrow road out of Limassol, past the ruins of Amathus towards Nicosia. Our destination was the Presidential Palace, where we would first tour the palace and gardens and then be received by Archbishop Makarios himself. Following that, we would cross the Green Line at the bottom of Ledra Street to visit the Turkish Quarter.

The Green Line was a narrow strip of territory which separated the two communities. To enter the no man's land between, you first had to pass by a Greek military post and then give proof of identity to Turkish soldiers on the other side. The United Nations had a position nearby keeping an overall watch over everything.

Unlike the situation in Limassol, where the Turkish Quarter was open and anyone could enter freely, the Turkish areas in both Nicosia and Famagusta were enclaved behind the old walled cities, and Greek Cypriots were denied entry. I had been inside the Turkish quarter of Nicosia once before. Stepping from the modern shopping area of Ledra Street into the Turkish-held territory behind the barricade was like taking a step back into the previous century. Buildings were crumbling and the roads were in a state of disrepair, but it was full of interesting sights and sounds and there were many unusual things to buy. Colourful cottons and other attractive materials could be purchased cheaply there and taken to one of the many seamstresses in Limassol, who could produce beautiful made-to-measure ball-gowns in one or two days. Apart from sight-seeing, which a few of us were keen on, this was the main reason for our visit.

Later we duly arrived at the Presidential Palace and were given a warm welcome by the Archbishop's personal secretary. While we toured the building and the beautiful gardens, he told me that an urgent situation had arisen. The Archbishop sent his most sincere apologies, but he would be unable to meet with us in person that morning. I told him I quite understood (frankly I had been pretty amazed he had said he would see us in the first place) and that it did not inconvenience us at all. We would have a little more time to spend in the

Turkish Quarter, I said.

A look of concern came over his face, and he asked me to step into the next room with him. He beckoned me through to the other side of the building where, outside, there seemed to be a lot of noise going on.

"I strongly urge you not to go near the Turkish Quarter this morning," he said. "There may be some trouble."

He indicated the road where a convoy of village buses was passing at some considerable speed. Clenched fists and arms holding guns, sticks and pitchforks were sticking out of the windows and there was a lot of shouting.

"The Turks are demonstrating this morning," he said.

I quickly loaded up my charges, and briefly explaining the situation to them, asked Ibrahim to stop at the nearest telephone box. I rang the Station Commander at Episkopi for advice.

"Good morning, Sir," I said brightly. "It's Sheila."

My reputation for disaster went before me. His reply was heartfelt and succinct: "Oh God," he said.

I enquired whether there really was a serious situation in Nicosia, because I had more than seventy British wives with me and we were on our way to the Turkish Quarter. He almost had a heart attack on the spot. It seems that Kurt Waldheim, the then Secretary General of the United Nations, was on an official visit to

Cyprus, and the Turkish Cypriots were mounting a militant demonstration for his benefit.

"Where are you now?" he asked.

When I told him, I had to hold the phone away from my ear.

"Get them out of there, and *do not* go anywhere near the Turkish Quarter," he replied forcibly.

"But what am I going to do with them all day?" I wailed piteously.

"I don't care what you do with them, just get them out of there."

I replaced the receiver and walked slowly across to the bus. Ibrahim took one look at my face.

"Grand mystery tour, Mrs Sheila?" he said.

6. THE BATHS OF APHRODITE

Following a routine visit to Headquarters at Episkopi, Harry came home to say that one of the clerical staff had invited us to a family celebration in a region we had not yet visited. It was on the north west coast of the island, not far from a small place called Polis. She came from a fishing family in an area famous for its fresh fish. It was also, she said, the most beautiful place on the island. We looked on the map to find Polis. It was certainly a fair distance away - given that there was no main road. The references we found said that only a small village now stood on the remains of two great former kingdoms - Marion and Arsinoe. Many rich artefacts had been discovered there, in fact buried treasure was uncovered practically every time someone dug a deep enough hole. It certainly sounded a fascinating place to visit, and we looked forward to the journey with anticipation.

We set off early on a warm and cloudless day. Driving unhurriedly along the narrow undulating route, we passed through Episkopi and on to the carefully tended vineyards of Pissouri. Beyond Pissouri, the landscape was spectacular - sparsely-vegetated limestone mountains and deep valleys looked like something out of a Hollywood wild west epic. The road dropped

We met a shepherd

steeply down towards the azure coastline and Petra tou Romiou - the legendary birthplace of Aphrodite. The morning sun highlighted the warm colours of the rocks and reflected off the white-painted hull of an upturned boat on the beach. The sea was flat calm, clear and brilliantly turquoise.

Wild goats roamed on the slopes, crossing and re-crossing the road in front of us. A little further along we met a shepherd leading his flock of sheep up from the beach. He greeted us with an upraised arm and we stopped to talk with him awhile. He was a handsome man with a white moustache and deeply tanned face. He congratulated us on having two children and proudly told us he had several children and grandchildren of his own. Delving into his bag, he produced a handful of shelled almonds and shared them with us. He then asked where we were going. When we told him he seemed surprised.

"But it is far away," he said.

We left him standing in the sunshine, his stick resting across his shoulders in a typical pose. The children waved from the back window until he was out of sight. There were few cars and no really heavy traffic to cause delays, and soon we were passing through Ktima and out on to the secondary road that led to Polis. At this junction another famous landmark was signposted, Loutra tis Aphroditis - the Baths of Aphrodite. The rough road twisted up the mountain through fields of carob and olive trees. On the high plateau, terraces were planted with grapes which supplied the big wineries in Limassol. As we descended towards sea-level once more, through *pervolia* planted with almond and plum trees, we were struck by how green the region was in comparison with other parts of Cyprus. Lower down, orange-groves planted in neat rows filled the wide riverbed, while the road ran on through citrus plantations and acres of land closely packed with olive trees. Suddenly, ahead of us, the blue Mediterranean danced and sparkled, and beyond we could see the mountains of the Akamas.

We drove into Polis. After a couple of hundred metres of interesting old buildings on either side of a narrow street, we came to a blue sign attached to a lamp-post in the middle of the road. In capital letters the words 'Town Centre' were accompanied by an arrow pointing to the right. We turned right, along another narrow street, and immediately found ourselves back where we had started. We were later to discover that the sign was positioned at the very centre of town. That was it. To be fair you could find everything you needed here. There was a coffee shop, a small market, a corner shop selling groceries, a bank, post office - even a small cottage hospital to serve the surrounding villages. It just seemed to be a bit of an insignificant place to be standing on the site of such former wealth and grandeur.

We made our way along a beautiful, unspoilt coastline to the little fishing port of Latchi, where a tiny stone-walled harbour gave shelter to several colourful fishing boats. A wooden pier jutted out, and some men were unloading a haul of sponges from a green boat which bore the inscription 'Tappas Divers'. There was a restaurant, a fisherman's abode, an old custom shed, and a carob barn, but apart from that there appeared to be no village of Latchi as such. We followed the track which led around the coast to the Baths of Aphrodite. It was truly an area of outstanding beauty. On our right a low white cliff marked one end of a glorious stretch of golden sand. Fields of corn, barley and other staple crops grew in the rich fertile soil on either side of the road, and carob and olive trees were plentiful. A diminutive shepherdess came by with a large flock of goats. In one hand she held a long stick, while under her arm she carried a new-born kid. A she-goat followed closely behind her, bleating plaintively. On one side of the road the overhanging branches of a huge carob tree provided plentiful shade for two honey-coloured oxen tethered in a field. They stood placidly chewing the cud, turning their heads to return our gaze with limpid, mournful eyes.

Finally we ran out of road, and there to greet us was Voulla. We walked with her to the edge of the cliff and looked down on to a small beach of multi-coloured pebbles lapped by water of the utmost clarity. A fishing boat was anchored in the little bay, and a young man who was sluicing the boards with sea-water from a red bucket waved to us. A large rock stood a little way off-shore. Plants clung to its surface in sheltered crevices,

A wooden pier jutted out

and minerals in its make-up coloured it pink and green. It was very unusual and quite beautiful.

A wooden fishing-shack had been built just below the top of the cliff, and here we were introduced to the rest of the family. They made us welcome in the typical hospitable way of the Cypriot - bringing cold drinks and plates of small pastries. Meanwhile, the morning's catch was being cleaned, potatoes were being peeled, and fresh salad was being prepared in readiness for lunch.

Some steep, roughly-hewn steps led to the little beach below and we picked our way carefully down. As we turned left at the bottom, we had to pass through a miniature jungle of tall bamboo grass and other lush vegetation growing where water was trickling towards the sea. Voulla explained that it was the overflow from the spring at the Baths of Aphrodite above, and she promised to take us there when we had eaten. We climbed over some rocks to where a rowing boat was moored in a small inlet, and to their great delight, the children were rowed around the bay by one of Voulla's cousins. Then, donning snorkel masks, they swam with him to be shown a large, orange-coloured starfish and the rock beneath which an octopus lurked. There were several species of small fish swimming around the rocky area, and they soon learned to identify them all with their Greek names.

Lunch was a feast indeed, and the view from our vantage point had to be seen to be believed. When we had eaten and rested, we walked the few hundred yards to the Baths of Aphrodite. On our right was a small headland dotted with carob trees, while on our left we could hear water splashing. Here there was an ancient Neolithic site - the name of which translated as 'Two Rivers'. To the right again was a goat trail, inaccessible by car, that meandered out on to the Akamas peninsula. Directly ahead, a mud and rock path led to the Baths. The narrow track was overhung with trees and shrubs, and on the right hand side the ground dropped steeply away into a ravine which was clothed in dense green vegetation.

The melodious sound of sheep-bells alerted us and we pressed ourselves against the rocks as a flock of sheep came towards us. They had been to drink at the spring and now plodded purposefully along in characteristic ovine manner - heads downcast and long tails bobbing behind them.

The path descended slightly and then we were at the Baths. This, legend had it, was where the Goddess Aphrodite used to come to bathe in seclusion. It was certainly a place of almost mystical beauty. A grotto, overhung with a trailing maidenhair fern, contained a pool of crystal clear water which was fed by a spring trickling down over the cliff. From here the water overflowed into a rock-cut channel and on down into the ravine, later to emerge on the little pebbled beach below. A wild fig tree spread its branches over the rocks, and our guide told us that in early spring wild cyclamen bloomed here in profusion.

Soon it was time for us to take our leave, and Voulla asked if we would give her a lift as far as Polis. Bearing left towards Latchi, I asked her where the road rising up on our right led.

"Nowhere of any interest," she replied. "Only the Akamas, but there are no roads to take you there past the one small village."

"What village is that?" I asked.

"Neo Khorio," she replied.

It was a name I was to remember.

* * * * *

Back in Limassol life continued at a brisk pace. On a personal level, I found myself perpetually occupied. There was so much to see and do, not to mention the little matter of the Wives Club to run, and a commitment to teach O level English Literature two evenings a week at the Education Centre. I didn't know it, but I was about to get busier. Harry came home to say the Group Captain in charge of SCEA would like to see me. SCEA stood for the Service Children's Education Authority, whose responsibility it was to ensure that service children, living overseas with their parents, received the same quality and diversity of education that would be available to them in the UK.

I turned up on time for the appointment, and almost before I knew it, found myself appointed

Schools' Swimming Instructor. Swimming pools were few and far between, and up until then, there had been no swimming lessons for pupils of the five English schools in Limassol. Now it was decided that, for the duration of the summer term, I would be stationed at Ladies' Mile beach and my students would be ferried down by bus. The swimming detail would arrive, one class at a time, with a couple of teachers in attendance to insist on orderly behaviour and to ensure that the number of children I returned to school corresponded with the number that had arrived in the first place.

I must admit that this was one of the best jobs I ever had. I was actually getting paid to stay on the beach all morning. The long, sandy length of Ladies' Mile was a safe place to swim. The water was clean, warm, buoyant, and no more than waist deep for a considerable way out. It was absolutely ideal for the teaching of swimming. The teachers acted as additional lifeguards and the children worked in pairs for safety reasons. It was, of course, a winner as far as the pupils were concerned - by far the most popular class in the school curriculum. I was rather sorry when the summer term ended!

The Limassol Adult Education and Training Centre continued to be a great success as more and more people enrolled for classes. A government Inspector's report equated Harry with two and a half civilians. Unfortunately we were never able to find out quite what half a civilian did, or even which half it was that did it.

The building was situated on the By-Pass near the crossroads which led down towards the main Police Station and up towards the village of Polemidia. The classrooms were on the first floor above a taxi office. Taxis were an essential part of everyday life, as few of the local population had cars. Fares were cheap and the drivers would go out of their way to find places that foreigners couldn't remember - or couldn't pronounce. While they waited for assignments, they sat drinking coffee and joking on a small paved area outside the entrance to the Centre. They were a friendly bunch, and we got to know them all very well.

Early one morning an old man was found wandering on the By-Pass. He was wearing the traditional *vraka* and walked with the aid of a crutch. He appeared to be bewildered and disorientated by the noise and traffic of modern-day Limassol. The drivers sat him on a chair and brought him coffee while they tried to find out where he lived. Harry, who took the opportunity to draw him as he sat there, said that the usually feisty characters who drove the taxis were extremely gentle and caring in their questioning of the frail old man. They made several phone calls and eventually discovered where he belonged. He had come down from a mountain village - apparently seeking his former house. But the small, quiet town he remembered had changed out of all recognition.

The drivers were kindness itself to this lost soul, and he was driven home in style in the back of one of

He was wearing the traditional vraka

the new taxis. I looked at the drivers' familiar faces with a new respect, having seen them in a different role. In the not too distant future I was to see them in yet another role - but I was not to know that then.

7. LIMASSOL

Social life continued at a hectic pace. Apart from Service functions on the bases, there was an endless round of eating out in Limassol. The big Turkish kebab houses like Niazi's, Mamhout's, Arif's and Halil's were popular with all British personnel and they were extremely competent in organising squadron events as well as catering for individual parties. Most, of course, were in or near the Turkish quarter itself. On the By-Pass, Scotti's steak house served the best steaks anywhere on the island, and further along, the amiable, amply-proportioned Gino produced magnificent pizzas and spaghetti bolognese in his small Italian restaurant.

Traditional Greek and Cypriot dishes were served at various mezze houses in town, and some memorable nights were spent in these establishments. The place we patronised most, however, turned out to be Chris Riverside. *Kokinelli,* that deceptively harmless sweet red wine, was served free at all eating places, but his was a local speciality and the quality of the food there was excellent. He was also a lively character and not averse to joining in the fun on occasions. In fact he was usually the first to start throwing plates on the raised dance-floor so that they were trampled, in truly

Greek fashion, by squadron members who were determined, at all costs, to keep pace with the bouzouki players. For years there was a kind of on-going competition between the British and the musicians. Every time they played 'Zorba the Greek' they tried, in vain, to see the dancers off the floor by speeding up their playing with amazing dexterity.

Chris Riverside restaurant was some distance out of town along the coastal road. From the harbour near the castle, the narrow road, lined on one side by numerous small workshops and old town houses with ornate balconies, followed the seafront towards Nicosia. Somewhere along here was one of the children's favourite venues - Délices. It was a café famed for its excellent cream cakes where, shaded by big sun-umbrellas, you could sit at small tables on the pavement nearest the sea and watch the waiters dodging traffic as they nipped across the road with their loaded trays.

Mimosa trees lined stretches of the coast and provided shade for beach-goers. Swimming was good, especially at Chez Nous just before the Municipal Gardens and Zoo. The Nautical Club was well-established, and a few open-air restaurants made for romantic moonlit dining on warm summer nights. The coastline generally, however, was mainly in an uncluttered and natural state. Out past the ETKO wine and the KEAN juice and soft-drinks factories there were open fields and trees, interspersed with a few restaurants and houses.

Further along, next to a country road leading up to the little village of Yermasoyia, was the restaurant known as Chris Riverside. From this point, the main road carried on to pass through the ruins of Amathus and on towards the capital, Nicosia.

A new hotel, the Apollonia, had recently been built - bringing the grand total, along the coastal stretch of road, to two. The Miramare was long established, but the new hotel had a lovely swimming pool and many of us became members of the recreational club, which gained us entry to the pool and bar whenever we wished. The number of hotels swelled to three with the construction of the big and modern Amathus. This one boasted a heated outdoor pool, and we often swam there on cool winter days.

As well as patronising the town's restaurants, we did a lot of entertaining amongst ourselves. Most of these occasions were pretty informal, and it was quite customary for someone you had invited to ask whether they might also bring their guests with them. I remember in particular one party we gave at Berengaria. An aircraft full of friends and relatives of service personnel had obviously landed at Nicosia International Airport the previous day, for the Doner kebab man, who was doing the catering for us, later told me that, in all, eighty-six people attended.

Some of these occasions proved more eventful than others. We went for supper one evening at a private house and the children, who were all playing in the garden, came rushing in babbling with excitement. They had spotted a small blue budgerigar perched in a tree. It was quite docile and offered no resistance when they picked it up. Enquiries were immediately made, but the owner could not be found anywhere in the neighbourhood.

"Please, please can we keep it - we'll look after it," chanted six or seven children simultaneously.

"No way," chanted three of the mothers, while I said nothing and wimpishly avoided my children's gaze.

My kids know a soft touch when they see one. My son, holding the tiny bird carefully in both hands, held it out and looked up at me - his deep brown eyes filling with tears.

"But it hasn't got anywhere to live. Who will look after it?"

Who indeed?

"We haven't got a birdcage," I said lamely.

"They're cheap enough to buy," interjected Harry, who is an even softer touch than me.

Our hostess, who had no intention of being lumbered, swiftly appeared beside me with a tray and a wire mesh thing, used to keep flies away from food as it cooled. It was a masterly piece of improvisation. When we left to go home, the children sat in the back of the car, one holding the tray and the other ensuring that no flies landed on the captive. The bird seemed perfectly at ease, while they chattered non-stop all the way. First they had to decide on a name, then they would work out how to get it to talk. They speculated on the content of its speech therapy, obviously believing the perfectly ordinary budgie had all the latent rhetorical genius of Winston Churchill.

Once home, we placed it high on top of the refrigerator, made sure the cat was out, and closed all doors and windows. In the morning, I promised, I would go downtown and buy a proper cage.

The following day, with Harry at work and the children at school, I cautioned Safia to keep the kitchen door closed - for inside we had a bird that was not securely caged. An hour or so later I returned with a large birdcage made of polished wood, some containers for water and food, a mirror, a bath, toys for it to play with, packets of seed... the shopping list was endless.

Safia was waiting at the door. I could see at once that something was wrong - she looked stricken. Behind her, in the kitchen, the tray and wire mesh cover were up-ended on the floor and a few bright blue feathers were scattered around. Beneath the table, a large cat sat contentedly licking its paws. I stared in disbelief. Yesterday I had a budgie with no cage. Now I had a cage with no budgie.

Safia, as requested, had kept the kitchen door shut, but had opened a fanlight high up on one wall. She never imagined a cat would be able to get anywhere near it. She reckoned without a determined character like Domino, though. He was a large neutered male whose pure white fur had one or two strategic black spots. He was an affectionate creature and extremely handsome, a bright red leather collar enhancing his unusual colouring.

He looked at me smugly and came to rub himself against my legs. Villain that he was, I could hardly blame him for ridding the kitchen of this strange blue intruder. Did I not regularly praise and reward him for his prowess at dealing with rats, mice and small snakes? He stalked majestically past me and stretched himself out to roll voluptuously in the dry earth beneath the fig tree. I wondered what on earth I was going to tell the children. While I was considering this terrifying prospect the telephone rang. It was one of the Vulcan pilots who said he'd be dropping by at lunchtime. I told him to be prepared for a few tears when the kids returned from school and discovered that the cat had helped itself to an early lunch.

"No problem," he said, "there are dozens of the things in the aviary down in the aircrew feeder. I'll bring one with me when I come."

The children came home from school and flung themselves upon the new cage - examining all the little accoutrements with delight. They dashed into the kitchen.

"Where's Sammy? Let's put him in."

I told them the truth. They were shattered and vowed never to speak to poor old Domino again. Their brimming eyes lit up, however, when I told them Bill was on his way for lunch with a replacement. Now I had gone to all the trouble of buying a cage, it seemed rather silly not to have something to put in it.

They looked at me with adoring eyes and I basked in their hero worship for a few minutes. Then Bill arrived on the back of Harry's small motorbike, and their faces fell as they saw he wasn't carrying anything with him. They looked at him beseechingly.

"Didn't they have any, Uncle Bill?"

"Any what?" Then, "Oh, you mean one of these things."

He delved into the pocket of his KD jacket and pulled out a small brown paper bag, with the top twisted like a bag of sweets. He opened it and peered in.

"He's a bit cross" he said, handing them the bag. Inside there was one unharmed, but furious, blue budgerigar. Having had its feathers seriously ruffled, the hijacked budgie was now installed in luxury accommodation of its own and given enough bird-seed to plant a field of millet. Then, screwing a large hook into a stout beam, Harry hung the cage up in the shade of the outside verandah where, safe from predators, Sammy, mark two, became a well-loved member of the family.

* * * * *

While life continued to treat the twelve thousand or so British families living in Limassol well, there was a growing discontent throughout the island. After years of colonial rule, Cyprus was an independent Republic.

Ardent followers of Colonel George Grivas, however, still yearned for enosis. President Makarios and the Colonel were no longer allies, as they had been during the struggle against the British, and a distinct division had arisen between the followers of each man. Those seeking change were becoming ever more militant. Propaganda leaflets were everywhere and gallons of blue paint were used up as more and more slogans were sprawled over every available wall. The blue and white striped flag of Greece was much in evidence - the new yellow and white emblem of independent Cyprus fluttering only over government buildings and police stations.

These now became the target of repeated attacks. Blowing up police stations was such a common occurrence that a massive explosion, shattering the silence of a summer evening get-together at our house, would cause only a raised eyebrow or two and a cryptic comment: "There goes another police station."

The hands of fate were beginning to cast dark shadows over Cyprus but, for us, life went on as normal. Limassol was very much our home town. We came to know every inch of it, making many friends as we went along. There were several unforgettable characters who were an integral part of daily life. One was a taxi driver whose pitch was outside the big church of Ayia Napa in St Andrew's Street. He was a huge, quintessentially Greek, man with a head of white hair and a fierce white moustache. His demeanour matched the moustache and his ancient green taxi was battle-scarred from countless encounters with walls and other vehicles. In our usual flippant manner we called him the Mad Bomber, and it was a brave (or too exhausted to care) passenger who stepped into his cab.

A blind man roamed the market area. He carried an ordinary stick and walked as rapidly as any sighted person - cannoning off the bumpers of parked cars and tripping over anything in his path. He carried a small tin mug and would lean against the wall of the market while passers-by dropped coins into it. The stallholders usually brought him something when they passed him. Most days he could be found surrounded with pieces of orange-peel as he sat on the pavement - legs outstretched and face turned up towards the sun. He recognised people by their voices and quickly came to know mine by its foreign accent.

Another crippled man rode around on an old tricycle, which had been adapted so that the pedals were raised and operated by hand. A wooden box, painted blue, had been built around him and in this he was able to put fruit, vegetables and other perishable goods he had been given at the end of the morning's trade. He too was glad of the coins given to him by shoppers and sightseers.

A boy of about twelve, suffering from Down's syndrome, wandered alone in the old town. He had a sunny disposition and seemed to be everybody's child. He went in and out of shops at will, and I never saw him

A blind man roamed the market area

receive anything but kindness and affection from everybody. We attended a big wedding once at the Ayia Triada church. The bride and groom were just having the coronets placed on their heads when the boy stepped up amongst the principal players and got in on the act. No one turned a hair. The officiating priest placed his hand gently on the child's head and carried on with the ceremony without faltering. It was a sight I have never forgotten: the packed church, richly embroidered robes, massed flowers and flickering candles. Incense swirled around the child's sweet face as he leaned against the priest - secure in the knowledge that he was loved. Here he felt at home. We had many times experienced their friendliness and hospitality, but in that moment I knew there was an inherent goodness and compassion in the Cypriot people.

Another memorable character usually to be found in the vicinity of the gymnasium when the children were let out of school, was Marcos. He was a kind of hermit. His long hair and beard were snowy white and he was a picturesque sight in a faded blue cotton tunic. Around his neck he wore a large wooden cross suspended on a leather thong. The senior pupils used to consult him, and for half a crown, it was said he would tell you if you were going to pass a forthcoming examination. He lived in a small one-roomed house next to a property which was enclosed by a high stone wall. In the garden behind the wall, a few nuns made honey and went about their daily business. We visited him a few

Around his neck he wore a large wooden cross

times, for Harry liked to photograph and draw him. On each occasion, if he heard the nuns speaking on the other side of the wall, he would leap to his feet and there would ensue some kind of altercation, with voices raised on each side. He would whack the wall with his stick as the argument became more heated. Eventually some kind of truce would be called, and he would return to sit with us as though nothing had happened. We never did discover what on earth it was all about.

Life was never dull in Cyprus. We had very quickly fallen in love with the physical beauty and ancient heritage of the island. Now we were feeling an increasing bond with its people.

8. THE PANHANDLE

For some time we had intended to make the journey to the end of the Panhandle to see the monastery of Apostolos Andreas. Legend had it that the Apostle Andrew, on a sea voyage to Jerusalem to attend the Feast of the Passover, restored the sight of a ship's captain who had previously had vision in only one eye. At the time, the ship was sailing past the extreme eastern tip of Cyprus, and the captain confided in him that they were desperately short of water. Andrew told him to drop anchor and send some of the crew ashore. There they would find drinking water. In this most unlikely rock-strewn place, they did indeed find wells of sweet water. The captain and crew, seeing these miracles, were instantly converted to Christianity and baptised by the Apostle.

When next he sailed past the island, the sea captain was reputed to have placed an icon of St Andrew by the source of the water. From this beginning grew the monastery, which became a place of great reverence for Greek Cypriots. Many Muslims prayed there too, for St Andrew was renowned for healing the sick. People made pilgrimage from long distances, seeking to be cured of their ailments. Those stricken with blindness, deafness and other seemingly incurable afflictions came by donkey, bus and taxi, or walked and trekked the endless miles in an act of faith. Such was their belief in the ability of the saint to work miracles. On the great Feast Days of the 15th of August and the 30th of November, thousands of pilgrims flocked to the monastery carrying gifts and candle-wax effigies of those who were too ill to make the journey.

It was a long way to Cape Andreas, and to have sufficient time to explore the area at leisure, we planned to break our journey and stay for a day or so in a small village, near the coastal town of Boghaz. The squadron rented a tiny house in Yerani for a minimal annual amount. You could book in advance to stay, needing only to check that no one else wanted it for the same period.

As was customary with us, we set off in the cool hours of the early morning. Our immediate destination was Famagusta, which boasted the only deep water harbour on the island. The town was famous for its miles of orange groves and well-kept gardens. Modern day Greek Famagusta had shops, hotels and a glorious stretch of sandy beach. It was known as Varosha and was a thriving commercial and tourist centre. In contrast, the old mediaeval city within the walls was a Turkish enclave. Inside the massive Venetian walls, the old city had a distinctly eastern flavour. It was mainly in ruins with narrow streets running haphazardly through the crumbling buildings. As in Nicosia, to step from the modern town outside into Turkish territory was like entering a time warp. The women were not veiled, but they wore headscarves and colourful cotton dresses. A man came by riding an ancient bicycle. He rode with one hand and, in the other, he held a large dark-coloured spherical object. A loud noise alerted me, and as he passed close by, I was amazed (and not a little alarmed) to see that he was actually carrying a swarm of bees.

The pace of life was unhurried. Street vendors were everywhere, but there was no noisy hustle and bustle and roar of traffic. Dominating the enclave was the Latin cathedral of St Nicholas. The Turks called this stunning piece of Gothic architecture St Sophia. They had added a minaret and it was in general use as the main mosque. There were two entrances to the old city. We entered through the huge archway of the land gate - impressive to a degree - notwithstanding its ongoing state of dereliction. It was the other entrance, however - the sea gate - that captured our interest and imagination. It was built by the Venetians in 1496 and the stonework had been faced with marble. Above the iron portcullis was a magnificent carving of a lion - the emblem of Venice. A legend surrounds this marble lion, and I first learned of it from Kevork K. Keshishian's marvellous guide book Romantic Cyprus, which we took everywhere with us on our travels. The legend says that once a year, sometime during the night, the lion opens its mouth wide for a brief period. Should anyone witness this phenomenon and put a hand down the lion's gaping throat, they will be rewarded with treasure of great value. As far as I know, the gold is still up for grabs.

Othello's tower beckoned. Built by the Lusignans, it was the former citadel of the city of Famagusta. Had this really been the inspiration for the scene of Shakespeare's Othello? No one knows for sure - the Bard writes only of the fortifications of "a seaport in Cyprus". Standing on the ramparts and looking at the city within the walls and the busy harbour area outside, made it easy to imagine, however, that this must have been the place.

We headed for the open road again. Cold chicken and quiche waited in the cool-box, and the warm sea looked inviting. A spell of rest and some swimming seemed indicated fairly soon. There was just one more place marked on our itinerary before we stopped for lunch. The sheer breathtaking beauty of the ruins of Salamis is difficult to describe. Pearly white marble columns rise up in front of a backdrop of golden sand and deep gentian blue sea. Here, archaeologists have uncovered untold riches and treasures. Gold, silver, glazed pottery and beautiful marble statues, among them Apollo, Aphrodite, Artemis and Hygeia.

For two thousand years Salamis was the leading kingdom of Cyprus and its main commercial centre. During its heyday it suffered occupation and revolt, sackings, fire and earthquake. The sun beat relentlessly down on the fallen stones and ancient capitals.

Pearly white marble columns

Sunbathing lizards turned their heads and scuttled for cover at our approach. Standing in the Palaestra, I felt a sense of unreality. Leaning against a marble column that had been smoothed by craftsmen many hundreds of years ago, I found it all too easy to imagine the generations who had walked there before me. An incredible mix of ancient peoples - among them Cypriot kings, Persian rulers, the Ptolemies of Egypt and the Romans. The very air had a sense of history. The overwhelming feeling of its greatness stayed with me while we swam in the clear water. Here somewhere, ships carrying salt, olive oil and copper had sailed on trade routes to Phoenicia and Egypt. How steeped in ancient cultures and civilisations was this lovely island.

At four o'clock, when the fierce heat of the sun had abated, we left the shelter of the big sun umbrella, and, cooled and refreshed by one last swim, went to seek out the monastery of Apostolos Varnavas. Apart from being a place of great historical interest, it was also home to three elderly monks who were renowned icon painters. Harry couldn't wait to see their work.

The Apostle Barnabas was stoned to death in Salamis by Syrian Jews who were opposed to the spread of Christianity. Later, his body was recovered and taken away for secret burial. In 478 AD a sepulchre containing his remains was found one mile west of Salamis. Inside the tomb was a copy of the Gospel of St Matthew in Barnabas' own handwriting. A stone-built mausoleum now stood over the ancient tomb, and we hoped

One was sitting at an easel

we would be able to go inside. First of all, though, we went to seek out the three monks in their studio. We had no idea how they would receive us. In the event, they gave us the warmest of welcomes. They were interested to learn that Harry was also an artist and proud to show him their work. They all had white hair and fine white beards. One was sitting at an easel and was happy for Harry to photograph him while he worked. He told us his name was Father Chariton and the others were his brothers, Barnabas and Stephanos. He himself was the eldest. They offered us coffee and we admired the accuracy and finish of the icons stacked against the walls. Before we took our leave, one of them elected to show us the tomb of St Barnabas.

Inside the dim cool interior of the mausoleum he led the way down some steps to the original cave - bidding us to take care. He told us there were fourteen steps leading down to a spring. Here the sick came to be cured by the holy water. It was particularly effective, he said, in the treatment of skin diseases.

It was a weird feeling to be standing in the very cave where one of Christ's Apostles was buried. I stood there, as if in a dream, listening to the soft hypnotic voice of the monk. There was so much I wanted to ask him, but my Greek was limited. He understood. He saw that I was moved and took my hand.

"O Theos mazi sou," he said, gently.

* * * * *

We drove eastward along the coast road to the seaside resort of Boghaz. It was late afternoon and a stiff breeze had begun to blow. The sea was intensely blue, and in the increasing swell a little armada of sailing dinghies tacked to and fro, dragging foaming wakes behind them. We turned inland and followed the narrow road a few miles to Yerani.

It was a small place, and the instructions we had been given were explicit. The tiny whitewashed house basked in the sunlight. It looked picturesque and inviting. We went in and looked around. It had everything you could possibly need, albeit the furniture was basic and rather sparse. A shower had been rigged up in the back courtyard, and the water in the tank was warm from the sun. It was nice to sit and relax after the full day of exploration. Opposite lived a shepherd who was apparently always keen to meet the British visitors. He came forward now with the traditional *"kopiaste"* and placed a few wooden rush-seated chairs in the road outside his house. His wife emerged with a small table on which she began to array a variety of dishes. There was *halloumi, fetta* and fresh *anari* which, she told us, she had made from their own flock's milk. She brought home-made bread, topped with sesame seeds, and plates with sliced tomatoes, small cucumbers, onions, and whole cloves of garlic. Her husband then produced a bottle of local brandy and another of *zivania.* He looked at us hopefully. The last people to stay in the house brought whisky with them, he said.

Harry nipped into the kitchen of our rented home and found in the cupboard a half-empty bottle of scotch. He would replace it with the one we had brought with us. It was the accepted thing to ensure there was always a supply of tea, coffee and other non-perishable essentials in the kitchen for the convenience of incoming visitors. Harry now put the bottle on the table and our neighbour's eyes lit up. I'm no connoisseur, but drinking malt whisky after being accustomed to *zivania* must be an uplifting experience. The shepherd, on his fourth tot, leaned back in his chair with a beatific expression on his face. He sat motionless in the same position for so long I thought he'd died and gone to Heaven.

We were up early the next morning. As we breakfasted, the sound of bleating and sheep-bells echoed through the house. The children dashed out to see what was going on. Outside the front door a large flock of sheep milled around. They were amazingly clean - their wool creamy white and curly. Most of the sheep we had seen were dust-covered from the clouds thrown up by their feet during their daily wanderings. Our neighbour told us he regularly took his flock down to the sea to clean their coats. He was extremely proud of his animals, which included several goats and a couple of well-behaved dogs.

His wife came out of their house carrying a low stool and a galvanised bucket. She seated herself and began to milk one of the goats. Her husband asked me whether I had ever milked a goat. I had, actually, but it had been a pretty poor attempt as I couldn't get the thing to stand still long enough for me to get a grip on things. The wife laughed merrily and stood up, offering me her seat. It was exceptionally easy, she indicated: a child could do it. My two little sneaks rapidly did a disappearing trick. They had a natural talent for spotting a forthcoming disaster that seemed to have skipped my generation.

The shepherdess smiled encouragingly and rattled the stool expectantly. There was nothing for it. I sat down. The goat immediately backed out of reach, but it was no match for the shepherd's determined wife. She yanked it back and jammed the bucket beneath its nether regions. I took a deep breath and, vowing to get my own back on my semi-hysterical family as soon as possible, grabbed hold of two leathery sausage-like appendages. The goat looked at me haughtily and stamped a hoof, tilting the bucket and spilling some of the milk already in there. I pulled and heaved, squeezed and shoved, but not a drop went into the pail. I relinquished my hold and the beastly thing took the opportunity to drop something which would have better been dug in around the roses right into the bucket. Its mistress roared her displeasure, and using both hands as a ladle she scooped the mess out of the milk. She then resumed her position and proceeded to milk the goat with no trouble at all. When she had finished she dipped a glass in the warm, frothy liquid and offered it to the children. They had seen the unwarranted additive, though, and they weren't having any. Me neither. I fervently hoped the milk she had used for the cheeses we had eaten the previous night hadn't suffered the same fate.

The ewes had all been milked and now the shepherd, whistling to his flock, set off down the road. We retraced our route to Boghaz, stopping only long enough to buy fresh supplies for a picnic lunch, before embarking on the long drive up the Panhandle to the very end of the island. On the way we planned to explore yet another fairytale castle.

Kantara is perched at some 2,000 feet, on the eastern end of the northern range of mountains. It was a steep drive and then no little climb to reach the ruins. The view from the top of the ridge literally took our breath away. You could see the sea on both sides, stretching in azure magnificence, for miles. To the south lay Israel and Egypt, and to the north was the southern coast of Turkey. It was a sobering thought to realise just how close to the massive underbelly of Turkey this small island lies.

On again up through the Karpas peninsula, past long beaches of fine golden sand, past rolling dunes tufted with marram grass and blooming with sea-daffodils. The sea, ever-changing from cerulean blue to turquoise, was fringed with white surf as breakers foamed in to hiss rhythmically up over the warm sand. It was a scene of

Kantara is perched at some 2,000 ft

magical colour and matchless natural beauty.

Then we were at the monastery. It was larger than I had anticipated, having had a church and many annexes added over the years. There were few people there, but a priest welcomed us and showed us around. It was quiet in this cool place, and it exuded a definitive air of reverence. In the church there were huge candles, some fashioned in human form. Underneath the modern-day buildings was a well contained in a small chamber. This, he said, was the original source of water around which the monastery had arisen.

Outside, it was an odd feeling to be standing right on the extreme tip of Cyprus. Offshore, a small group of rocky islands, the Klides, stood guard - jutting from a sea which stretched into ultramarine infinity.

The rest of the day was ours to savour and relax. We returned to Chelones, the glorious beach which took its name from the hundreds of sea-turtles that came ashore there to breed. Here, we enjoyed our picnic lunch and frolicked in the surf. It was a veritable paradise - like being on a desert island. We met no one and saw no human footprints other than our own. In the late afternoon we headed back towards Yerani, diverting here and there to explore interesting bits of territory. Shortly before sunset, we came upon a lovely inlet surrounded with shapely white rock, smoothly sculpted by the sea. We stopped, for here the setting sun would provide a magnificent display. The sea swirling by the rock was crystal clear with an almost emerald hue. The children dived and swam and clambered out like seals, their white-blonde hair slick and wet. They called out in excitement as a pelican, in ponderous flight, passed low ahead before dropping to settle gently on the water.

A hush fell as the sky, blushed at first with rosy tints, glowed red, streaked with copper and bronze. Then, suddenly, the world around us was bathed in gold. It was one of those rare moments when time seems to stand still. Entranced, I could only stare at the children sitting, like gilded statues, on wet white rocks while out in the bay the pelican floated on a sea of golden sequins.

9. ESCAPE FROM THE WIVES CLUB

The weeks swept by, with Harry too busy to take more than a few days' leave at a time. He intended to apply for block leave at the end of his three-year tour, so that we could visit the Lebanon, Egypt, Israel, Syria and Jordan before we returned to England. Political unrest continued on the island, but Archbishop Makarios seemed firmly in control. In this he had the help of the United Nations, whose peace-keeping troops were stationed at various flashpoints. In those places where trouble was most likely to occur, Greek and Turkish troops warily watched each other and the UN carefully watched them both. Meanwhile, EOKA was becoming ever more militant in denouncing Makarios and the status quo. It was a potentially explosive situation, but the bulk of the population carried on with their daily lives regardless. Nothing serious could come of it. After all the United Nations forces were here and there were three guarantors - Great Britain, Turkey and Greece itself. What could possibly happen?

What indeed?

My stint at the Wives Club continued with no real improvement in the percentage of disaster days.

Even the carnival float, which received such wild applause from the local people and which won a special award, came to a sticky end. Dressed as St Trinian schoolgirls, in gym-slips and waving hockey-sticks, the British girls were being transported in the grand carnival parade in an open army lorry. The tailgate was down and two or three of them were sitting with their legs dangling over the edge. The procession moved at a crawl, stopping and starting according to the progress being made ahead. Then, at one stop, the following vehicle failed to brake in time and ran into the back of the float. Fortunately, there was no real speed involved and, thankfully, the tailgate had not been fixed - so their legs were not crushed as they might have been. One or two of the girls were badly bruised, however, and it spoiled the day for us all.

Some mishap or other inevitably occurred at the weekly meetings and, as for the away trips, Ibrahim was beginning to run out of ideas for his grand mystery tours. With hindsight, I can't think why on earth I didn't get him to fix the venues in the first place - it would have saved us all a lot of trouble.

We even had a near riot on a hen night in a Turkish kebab house. My second-in-command told me that the wives were all in favour of a night out without their husbands. Moreover, she was well-acquainted with the proprietor of an establishment who would give them a very good deal for a large party. In appreciation of the fun they all had, wondering what would go wrong next at my meetings, they would like to invite me to attend as their honoured guest. I arrived at the Moonlight kebab house, to find an air of expectation and around sixty ladies, dressed to the nines and seated at several long tables. A seat had been reserved for me in the centre somewhere and I was warmly greeted. Taxis and lifts home had been organised. The girls were husband-free and unfettered for the night. Nothing was going to stop them from having a good time.

The Turk who ran the place had hired a few extra waiters for the occasion and the first of many carafes of free *kokinelli* soon appeared on the table. I have to say the traditional kebab that followed was excellent and the atmosphere was happy and gregarious. There was a great deal of giggling at a short, stout Turkish man who, it must be said, was some way past his prime. He stood in the kitchen doorway the whole evening, simply staring at the girls. When the last of the courses had been cleared away, the waiters brought bowls of fresh fruit and dishes of Turkish Delight. A fair amount of *kokinelli* had been downed by this time, and when a tape of some Turkish music was put on, one or two of the more adventurous got up and began to dance.

At last the watcher in the doorway was galvanised into action. He grabbed a tumbler, half filled it with the red wine and balanced it on his head. Bending his knees, he then began a fantastic gyration - whirling around without spilling a drop. This was the point at which things began to go wrong. One by one the wives decided to have a go. The waiters readily filled the glasses and put them on their heads to start them off. The Turk who had performed the dance in the first place, now stood by with a broom and, every time a glass toppled from someone's head and shattered on the floor, he stepped in and gaily swept the pieces to one side. It all began to get a bit out of hand. I've never seen so many dripping beehive hairdos in my life.

It was at this point that I, somewhat hastily, took my leave.

"See you on Tuesday," they all shouted as I left. The ultimate optimist, I was taking them to a modern dairy farm on our next outing. I use the word optimist advisedly, for to be truthful, none of us had ever seen a cow anywhere near Limassol. Yet the Charalambides dairy had a tiny office on the By-Pass where you went to pay the monthly milk bill and get a small handbook marked by the girl who kept the accounts. They must get supplies from somewhere, I reasoned, and what about the letter I had received from this firm, inviting me to bring my ladies to visit their modern dairy farm? I re-read the letter. It was well-written, typed on the firm's headed notepaper and properly signed and dated. I told myself not to worry.

Tuesday dawned sunny and hot. We loaded up two coachloads of ladies - all looking forward to their day out. I rode in the first bus with Ibrahim who, although purporting to know the way, kept shaking his head in a woeful manner. I ignored his pessimistic attitude and clutched my letter for comfort.

The bus turned off the main road and bumped up a dry-mud track. We turned in through two gateposts which had the gate between them missing. My spirits began to take a nose-dive. I come from the lush green dairy-farming county of Devon, and this did not look a lot like a dairy farm - modern or otherwise. There was not a cow in sight - nor yet one blade of grass. Not even a dried cow-pat. There were one or two roughly fenced-in areas of bare earth and a few deserted outbuildings, but no milking sheds festooned with stainless steel machinery, humming with activity and brimming with milk. No sound of cows lowing or bulls bellowing. In fact, there was no sound at all as my troops got down from the coaches and tried to find some shade.

I glanced desperately across at Ibrahim. He raised his shoulders and rolled his eyes up towards Allah. There was a courtyard and a single-roomed, white-washed house across from one of the fenced areas. I strode purposefully forward and called loudly *"Kali mera"*. To my amazement there was a faint response. A weak voice urged me to come in. I pushed back the partly-open door and found myself looking at a man lying in bed. He looked a bit pathetic and I asked him if he were ill. At this, he raised the dingy sheet that covered him to show me his leg was in plaster.

"Ime poli arostos," he said with heartbreaking pathos.

The grubby plaster was bad enough, but I couldn't take my eyes off the huge cockroach that was crawling over it. I backed up a step and hung on to the door lintel as I explained my predicament. He pointed to a telephone on a table and told me to ring the number on the letterhead. It was a number in Nicosia. I rang and, after speaking to just about everyone else they employed, eventually got to the manager who had sent me the letter. I told him that, at his invitation, I was here with some eighty British ladies, who were rather hot and not too pleased at the situation in which they now found themselves. Speaking excellent English, he assured me that if we would be patient a little longer all would be resolved.

What he failed to tell me is that we had to be patient while he drove all the way down from Nicosia. He arrived in a swirl of dust just as I was wondering whether I would soon have a mutiny on my hands. I stepped forward to greet him, thankful that things were moving at last. His opening gambit was one of pure genius.

"Welcome to our modern dairy farm. We haven't actually got any cows, but I can show you where they were."

I smiled my disbelief at his little jest - but he was deadly serious.

"It is the government's fault," he said. "They passed a law that milk has to be pasteurised. Now all the cows are kept in Nicosia so they can be tested regularly by the inspectors."

I didn't have the heart to ask why he hadn't mentioned this trifling item when inviting us to the Limassol venue.

"Haven't you any animals at all?"

"Well," he replied, "we do have four or five calves being reared here."

My hopes slightly raised at having at least something to look at, I followed him to one of the outbuildings some distance away. Inside were four lethargic calves - long since weaned. They looked up disinterestedly when we entered. He poked one and it moved a few steps.

"They have their exercise sometimes," he explained apologetically, "But the farmer here has broken his leg."

I told him the latter point had not escaped my attention. I briefly thought of asking him to send the animals, one by one, around the building for the benefit of the waiting wives. If we chased them fast enough they might get the impression it was a whole herd of them. I dismissed the thought as being silly almost as soon as it came into my head, and taking the bull by the horns, went back to tell my ladies the truth. Real troupers that they were, a great roar of laughter went up. We then spent an entertaining three minutes seeing where the cows had once been and another two looking at the mangy calves.

For a finale, the manager triumphantly played an ace. He opened the boot of his car and proceeded to distribute small bottles of warm milk to us all. He then got into his car and zoomed off down the track. There was still a great deal of time left before we were due back - I'd have to come up with something. I turned towards Ibrahim, but he was already climbing resignedly up behind the wheel. I wondered where today's mystery tour would take us. In the event it was to a small Turkish village where, said Ibrahim, they really did have a cow. He knew this for a fact because his uncle, who was a shepherd, kept one.

We found the shepherd squatting in a characteristic pose in the doorway of his house. He appeared somewhat bemused by the sudden appearance of such a large number of foreign women, but rose magnificently to the occasion. He did indeed have a cow. He also had sheep, goats, rabbits, pigeons, hens, turkeys, geese and a donkey with a foal. The wives were delighted. They picked up furry little rabbits, stroked the donkey foal and ooh-ed and aah-ed over little white lambs and new-born kids. Ibrahim smiled smugly. We'd had a longer journey than expected, but he had saved the day again and it was a whole lot more fun than the dairy-farm anyway.

* * * * *

Although I did not know it then, a golden opportunity was about to come my way. An officer's wife who would be living in Limassol was soon to arrive on the

Squatting in a characteristic pose

island. Moreover, she was an avid supporter of Wives Clubs and had indicated she would like to become involved in this one. I meticulously planned my escape. She arrived at the beginning of November and readily agreed to a hand-over in the near future. The ideal occasion for this soon presented itself. A Christmas dinner-dance had been organised at the Astir, which was then one of the most popular hotels in town for private functions. The big feature of this dinner was to be a dress show, which would take place while dessert was being served. A local boutique had undertaken to supply the dresses, models and compère. The hotel would provide a changing-room for the models and construct a raised catwalk extending out into the dining-room from the bottom of the mezzanine stairway. Evening dress would be worn, there was an excellent menu and the hotel's resident trio would play throughout. For once, I didn't have to get involved. The committee had it all organised with the boutique. I would be able to dine, dance and enjoy myself.

The big night arrived and we turned up with my farewell speech tucked in Harry's pocket. Tonight I was going to go out in style. I'd had my fill of disasters. Or so I thought. The first inkling I had that everything was not running smoothly was when a panic-stricken committee member skidded to a halt behind my chair just as I was about to tuck into the roast turkey.

"We're two models short," she wailed.

"OK. What sizes are the dresses?"

"We need a 10 and a 12."

I stood up and surveyed the scene, then advanced on two likely volunteers and dragged them away from their dinner, with a promise I'd get the kitchen staff to feed them later. The committee member didn't go away. I looked at her.

"We haven't got a compère," she whispered.

"What do you mean you haven't got a compère?"

"She's gone to Israel, All we've got are her notes with the description of the dresses."

I glanced at the notes. They were neatly written and in good English.

"OK, one of you stands by the band, holding the hand-mike, and reads from the notes as the models come down."

An expression of terror came over her face.

"We *can't*. None of us has the nerve in front of all these people."

"OK, OK. I'll do it. I'll read through the notes while I eat. Are you sure the dresses you have are the same ones listed here?"

"Yes."

"Well, for God's sake make sure you send them down in the same order so I don't make an idiot of myself describing the wrong ones when they waltz down the mezzanine stairs."

She still didn't go away. I looked at her with increasing dread.

"Please tell me nothing else has gone wrong. What other disaster could possibly befall us at this stage?"

"The models' changing-room is two floors up and the lift doesn't stop at the mezzanine."

That floored me momentarily. Then, desperately trying to gather my wits, I excused myself from the table, walked sedately out of the room, then tore up to the changing-room. It was crowded with women, in various stages of undress, being fussed over by dressers, hairdressers and somebody holding a long strip of safety-pins. They all seemed in good spirits, not yet having realised how fast they were going to have to move. I hoped they were all fairly athletic and steady on their feet.

The show had been planned so that the models would first appear in view of the audience halfway along the mezzanine floor. Here they would be announced before gracefully descending the staircase on to the catwalk and waltzing out into the midst of the diners. However, no one had thought to check out beforehand how exactly they were going to arrive at the head of the stairs - or indeed how long it would take them to do so. In fact, they had to come down one full flight of stairs and across the considerable length of the mezzanine itself to get there. Having minced down and done their stuff on the catwalk, they had to slowly climb the stairway again and cross the part of the mezzanine which left them in full view. Then they had to dash up the stairs to get changed into their next outfit - trying to avoid tripping over the next model coming down.

This, of course, threw the timing of the whole thing into confusion. Dessert was about to be served and I was about to be thrown in the deep end. I grabbed the microphone and mentally wished the boutique owner a rough crossing. No wonder she'd gone to Israel.

The first girl had no problem to begin with. She simply came down the stairs, crossed the mezzanine and stood poised at the head of the stairway. I duly introduced her by name and described her dress as she swayed along the catwalk and back up the stairs. She passed the second girl halfway along the mezzanine, then began to quicken her pace. As soon as she was out of sight, she began to run, her high heels beating a loud tattoo on the polished wood floor. It rapidly deteriorated from then on. There was no way they could swan along in supermodel style and get in position in the time available. Eventually I decided the best thing to do was make a joke of it. All eyes were turned upwards towards the head of the stairs awaiting the arrival of the next model and, in one of those sudden hushes that appears, the sound of her footsteps as she hurtled across the upper floor could clearly be heard. I switched on the mike as she came into view.

"And here we have Angela, thundering along the mezzanine floor in yellow silk-taffeta...."

Taking it in good part, she did a twirl and a curtsey at the top of the stairs and got some rapturous applause from the audience who, fortunately, saw the funny side of the situation. Thereafter, I ad-libbed in similar vein until all the dresses had been shown. Come the end, I was quite enjoying it myself.

Before the dancing began, I formally handed over the Wives Club to the next Chairman. They had all clubbed together to buy me a gift and said so many nice things about me that I suddenly felt too choked to give my prepared speech. Harry, always the professional, saw my predicament and came to the rescue. He stood up and immediately gained everyone's attention with his opening remarks.

"I have been asked to propose a toast to my wife's success. However, I have to say that over the past months I have been increasingly mystified by this phenomenon. I can understand someone organising a flower-arranging with no flowers, or even going to see oranges being packed when there are no oranges. But how the hell anyone can go to a dairy farm with no cows is beyond me. Nevertheless, despite the fates being less than kind to her on occasion, there are many ladies here tonight who have seen a great deal more of the island than they would have done otherwise. The grand mystery tours of the Limassol Wives Club are famed beyond these shores and that, in itself, is deserving of a toast."

He smiled at me and raised his glass.

"To Ibrahim," he said.

10. THE BACK OF BEYOND

Spring arrived, and Daphne, the wife of the proprietor of the bar where we held our meetings, telephoned. She was a tall, elegant woman and she spoke excellent English. We had become friends during my time with the Wives Club and I knew she had a house in the country somewhere. Now she was ringing to invite us there for the weekend. It was, she said, in the most beautiful of places. They intended to open up the house, water the garden and cook *souvla* for lunch. I asked where the house was and she told me it was at Neo Khorio. I remembered the name at once. It was the village we had not had time to explore on the day we had gone with Voulla to the Baths of Aphrodite. We gladly accepted the invitation and looked forward to visiting that lovely part of the island once again.

As was our custom, we set off early - arranging to meet our hosts by the carob barn in Latchi at eleven o'clock. We made our way to Asprokremma to explore the beach. The long golden stretch was made up of fairly coarse grains of sand and tiny multi-coloured stones. Clear, deep water, in emerald and turquoise hues, gurgled around the promontory of the low cliff. At the top, wild anemones bloomed in profusion with yellow rockroses and sweet-scented broom. In crevices among the flat rocks, wild cyclamen raised fresh and delicate flowers above heart-shaped leaves.

The land leading towards the Baths, on either side of the road, had fertile red soil - much of it planted with spring wheat and barley. Everywhere looked lush and green. On the left, the ground rose up towards the village of Neo Khorio. A circular lime kiln stood on one slope. It was obviously no longer used, for many of the stones had fallen and were crumbling into decay. Straight ahead were the mountains of the Akamas. We wondered what mysteries might lie beyond them.

We met up with Daphne and Andreas at the old stone-built carob barn, and followed them up the hill towards the village. Before we encountered any houses, we turned left up a narrow and pitted track, which was more like an old river-bed than a road. Andreas had been born in this region and the house was built on some of his family land. One day, he said, he would rebuild it into a modern, luxurious home, for he felt happier here than he did living anywhere else.

It was a clear day and the view from the verandah was breathtaking. The house stood above an orange plantation in acres of ground surrounded by carob, olive, pine and eucalyptus trees. Much of the steeply-sloping ground was covered in juniper bushes and flowering broom, beneath which pink rock roses and wild orchids bloomed. A steep gorge marked one boundary and the pine and cypress trees, which clothed its sides, were part of the ancient Akamas forest.

Wild cyclamen raised fresh and delicate flowers

The flat plain below was verdant with spring wheat and the tiny stone-walled harbour at Latchi was bathed in bright sunlight. The sea was vividly blue, lapping a long beach of golden sand which curved around the bay to meet a small forest on the outskirts of Polis Chrysochous. A few houses nestled on the opposite shore, against a backdrop of mountains which swept down to the point at Pomos.

There was work to be done before lunch. While the children collected brushwood for the fire, Harry helped Andreas to water the trees. Daphne and I walked a few hundred metres up the track, past an almond grove glorious with pink and white blossom, to pick *glysteritha.* This was a succulent edible plant, sold in bunches in the market place together with parsley and other greenery. As well as being nutritious, it had a subtle flavour and was an excellent accompaniment to salads. Daphne knew a slope where the plant grew profusely. We gathered a basketful with ease, although the land was not easily penetrable - being covered in thorn bushes and woody shrubs as well as carob trees. A point of hard rock stood prominently out and I climbed on to it to admire the view. From here it was even more beautiful than it was from their house. The tree-covered sides of the valley framed the bay like a magnificent landscape painting.

I stood on the rock wondering if I had ever seen anything more spectacular and beautiful in my life. When Daphne called, I found it difficult to tear myself away - it was such a magical spot in the middle of nowhere. I turned to go, mentally vowing to come here again. I was enchanted with this untamed piece of land, but had no idea that I was in the very place where, more than a decade later, our future home would stand.

* * * * *

Political unrest on the island grew. Back in Berengaria Safia voiced her concern. She was afraid for her children should trouble arise. She indicated a neighbour of hers, a sad-looking Turk dressed in traditional *vraka,* who walked down the narrow lane beside our house every day. She told me his son had been killed in a previous outbreak of ethnic violence. He was so devastated by the event that from then on he was never again seen with his head raised. He walked always with eyes downcast and head bowed. I did my best to reassure her, but if the truth were to be told, I had severe misgivings of my own at the way things were going.

Meanwhile, for us, life continued as normal, with parties and get-togethers in various locations. The Vulcans used to fly on a regular basis to Mazirah. The crews dubbed this flight 'the fish run', because they always brought back fresh barracuda steaks and crayfish with them. One night Bill decided a crowd of us were going to barbecue some of this delicious seafood, and at the same time, learn how to play Mah Jong. He had brought back a few sets from Singapore some weeks earlier. They were in attractive carrying-cases, and the salesman had assured him the full instructions were inside.

We had a sumptuous meal and then settled round the green baize-covered games table. As it happened, none of us had any idea at all how to play the game.

"Never mind," said Bill. "These sets come complete with written instructions."

They did indeed. But when we opened the booklets, they were all written in Chinese.

Harry was by now an honorary member of 35 Squadron which, as one of its unofficial duties, sponsored a Cheshire children's home in Addis Ababa and was always looking for ways to raise money. He drew a portrait of a local priest and it was framed and raffled at the Summer Ball. It generated such a lot of cash, and so many people wanted one like it, that someone came up with the idea that we should go into print with similar line drawings. Some could be made into cards and notelets for various squadrons. They would be a great aid to fund raising at summer fêtes and Christmas bazaars.

With this in mind, Harry began to photograph local scenes and people he felt he would like to draw. He particularly loved the older residents whose faces were full of character. Most of them enjoyed the novelty of having their picture taken, but one or two we encountered did not. We always asked first - not wishing to be

A sad-looking Turk

rude or to offend anyone. Sometimes, however, it was impossible to seek permission if the subject was part of a passing scene which might quickly disappear. It was on one of these occasions that Harry came seriously unstuck. Driving through Polemidia one day he suddenly stopped the car and leapt out, camera at the ready, having spotted an old Turkish woman riding a donkey with loaded pannier baskets. He took a couple of shots while her attention was distracted. When she noticed him, she spurred her mount forward with surprising energy and, advancing on him, she began to belabour him with her stick. He weaved and ducked out of the way while she yelled and swiped at him. Then the donkey joined loudly in the protest. It was sheer pandemonium for a moment or two. The very angry lady continued to upbraid him long after he was out of her reach and diving for the safety of the car. I have no idea what she was saying, but somehow I don't think she was enquiring after his health. He wasn't too pleased with me. I really would have opened the door for him, but I couldn't move for laughing.

In July Harry took a few days leave and we went to Kyrenia. He had plenty of film and two or three sketch-pads with him, hoping to find suitable material for his drawings. Much to the children's delight, we stayed in a caravan at Snake Island Beach. It was one of their favourite venues and a marvellous place to relax. We hired a boat and chugged along the azure coastline, stopping to swim in the clear, warm water at will. By

While her attention was distracted

car we explored isolated villages and sought out old Byzantine churches. They were golden memorable days but underneath the normalcy there was a growing sense of unease.

We kept in touch with events by listening to BBC world service and BFBS on the car radio. The political situation worsened, and after a few days we decided to cut short our stay and return to Limassol with the children.

On Sunday we went to see some friends who had bought a small house in the village of Lania. Michael Owen was an artist who was gradually making a name for himself, and his wife, Jacky, was an accomplished teacher of classical ballet. Their new house would later become the first art studio in Lania and they were busy making interior improvements without spoiling its traditional village style.

They had acquired a docile old donkey called Harold and the children rode him bareback. They sat astride, one behind the other, and waited for Michael to give him a nudge. The obliging beast would then plod slowly around the village and make his way back again with no further urging. His riders, of course, couldn't get enough of this.

Dusk fell and we sat in the garden enjoying the peaceful atmosphere. It was a perfect night. A big yellow moon rose over the mountains, bathing the pine-covered slopes in its radiance. Small bats flitted overhead and the warm air was scented with jasmine. There was no sound other than the soft calling of owls and the steady clopping of Harold's feet on the cobblestones. We remarked on their idyllic situation and the beauty of the surrounding countryside. Michael turned towards me and asked why we didn't get ourselves a similar village house before we returned to England. There were plenty available and they were certainly affordable. They did not take my reply seriously, but it came back later to haunt us. Now, almost a quarter of a century later, whenever we meet we tend to recall the occasion and my unwittingly prophetic remark.

"I have a feeling the whole situation on the island is going to blow."

The very next day, July 15th 1974, the Presidential Palace in Nicosia was attacked and the coup that would have such a devastating effect on the island was launched.

11. COUP D'ETAT

At about seven-thirty on that fateful morning, before we had any idea that anything was seriously wrong, I drove our Saab 99 down to a garage on the edge of the Turkish quarter, where it was to be waxed and polished ready for transportation back to the UK. Harry's three-year tour of duty was due to end in August, and once the car had been shipped, we would have use of a *gizzit* until we left the island. We had a lot of leave stored up and were planning our itinerary to visit several Middle Eastern countries which were practically on our doorstep. I left the car in the garage with Elias and waited in the coffee-shop across the road for Harry to come and pick me up on his small motor-bike. By the time he arrived it became apparent that something of major importance was going on. There was a buzz of activity all around us. Groups of anxious people began to gather. Then the incredible news rippled through the town.

Makarios is dead.

We drove to the Education Centre through swelling crowds now thronging the streets. Many of the women were weeping openly. Harry contacted RAF Episkopi to be told a movement had taken place in Nicosia to overthrow Archbishop Makarios, but that the overall situation remained unclear. A massive traffic-jam began to build up on the By-Pass and normal life came to a standstill. Over the next few hours varying accounts of what had taken place filtered through. It appeared that the National Guard had carried out a military coup. The Presidential Palace had been attacked and Archbishop Makarios had been killed.

The news stunned the population. Attempts had been made on his life before. In 1970 his helicopter had been shot down but he had walked away from the wreckage unharmed. Many of his supporters looked upon him as a kind of saint. He had been with them through the uprising against the British. They had kept him in their hearts during his enforced exile in the Seychelles until, unscathed, he had returned in triumph to his beloved Cyprus. They had believed he was invincible. Now came the shocking news that, this time, he had not survived.

At about nine-thirty we heard firing close by. It came from the area around the main police station which was only a few hundred metres down the road from the Centre. Soon, National Guard supporters wearing combat gear and carrying guns were everywhere and the rattle of automatic weapons increased. Men who normally drove lorries and delivery vans around the town were now wearing uniforms and riding shotgun on their vehicles.

The Turks set up a barricade of oil drums, barbed wire, concrete blocks, lorries and cars and sealed themselves inside the Turkish quarter. British families living outside the Sovereign Base areas were placed under curfew. Harry closed up the Centre and we weaved our way through the traffic up to Berengaria. That night we slept little as we listened to the battle raging in the town below us. Firing was non-stop and the clear night sky was patterned with high calibre tracer bullets.

As dawn broke, intense firing was concentrated on the By-Pass in the area around the central families office at Unicorn House and the Education Centre. Heavy fighting continued throughout the island on the 16th of July. On the afternoon of the 17th there came a lull, during which convoys from Episkopi and Akrotiri were hastily arranged to get living-out servicemen back to their families in Limassol. Many wives had tales of encounters too close for comfort. Some had suffered frightening experiences trying to retrieve their children from schools in the town when fighting had broken out on the first day. As usual with British Service wives though, morale was high.

All hirings housing Service families in and around Limassol were marked with a red strip and each sector of the town had a warden responsible for all the families in his area. In time of trouble the Station Defence Liaison Officer, operating from Unicorn House, would rely on his wardens to know the location of each hiring and the whereabouts of the occupants.

On the 17th the curfew on British families was

lifted for a few hours to enable people to get essential supplies. With the situation unstable and the outcome unforeseeable, Harry decided we had better get the car back during this relatively quiet period, whether it was ready or not. Armed with a Union Jack and several stickers, we set off for the garage on the small motor-bike. We turned into an empty street to see a man crossing the road further down. Another man, stepping forward from the shadows, lifted a gun and shot him. He fell to the ground and lay there. It was like watching a scene played out on television, but this was real. We did an about turn and took another route. When we reached the garage, Elias was polishing the wax off the car and laughed at the notion there might be worse to come. Nevertheless, he would be finished in twenty minutes or so. I photographed him and his brother as they worked.

Harry went to the Education Centre to check whether it was all secure and how much damage had occurred. Elias ordered me a cup of *metrio.* I sat outside the coffee-shop on the other side of the road, sipping my coffee and watching two old men playing backgammon in the shade. Suddenly there was a rattle of automatic fire and everyone quickly disappeared inside - save me and the two backgammon players who were engrossed in their game. The *kafejis* came out and beckoned me urgently inside, shouting to the two old men to get in as well. They calmly picked up the box, went in and carried on with their game. More gunfire erupted, but they simply ignored it while everyone else hit the floor.

The rough building was only semi-constructed from cement blocks and did not provide a lot of cover. So, at the sound of shouting and more shooting outside, I thought it prudent to duck beneath the open space where the windows would eventually go. I felt extremely foolish lying in the dust among the coffee-shop's clientèle and was dying to see what was going on outside. I heard a heavy vehicle screech to a stop and a thud as something was evidently thrown into it. At this I couldn't resist sticking my head around the corner of the wall. I was still holding my small camera but, before I could get in a position to photograph anything, a hand reached down and gently removed it from my grasp.

I looked up to see a man in civilian clothes carrying an automatic rifle. He held out his hand and helped me to regain my feet. He did not smile, but brushed the dust from my arms and courteously handed me back the camera.

"We mean you no harm," he said in excellent English, "but it is better if you stay inside."

He stepped through the doorway. I heard a car door slam. A motor gunned and an over-revving vehicle roared away. After that the silence was tangible. Then it was as if nothing had happened. The *kafejis* brought me a fresh coffee, the two old men continued their interminable game of backgammon, and a hum of conversation broke out again.

I crossed the street, relieved to find there were no bullet holes in our nice new car. I paid Elias. He grinned. He didn't even mention the incident. I stuck a few identifying stickers on the windscreen, and with the British flag fluttering from the partly-closed passenger window, made my way slowly home. I passed through several road-blocks manned by armed men who examined my passport and waved me politely on. I recognised many of them. It was difficult to believe that only a day or so earlier they had been going about the usual daily business of delivering milk and driving taxis.

The curfew was reimposed at two o'clock that afternoon, and for the next two days we were confined within the retained site at Berengaria. All families were in the same boat and we made the best of it, feeling ourselves to be luckier than those stuck in their sometimes isolated hirings in the town. An almost party atmosphere prevailed. We shared the contents of our freezers with each other, and with no fresh supplies available, several of us had a go at bread-making. Each evening became a social event with the children all playing together while the adults amused themselves with card games and invented outrageous cocktails from the partly-used bottles in the drinks cabinets.

Meanwhile we listened intently to the British Forces radio. From here came up-to-the-minute news of the situation and instructions to all military personnel and their dependants. On Friday the 19th of July there were strong rumours of invasion. The British High Commission broadcast a warning message to all British Nationals living in Cyprus and to the large number of holiday-makers spread throughout the island. Troops had been massing on the southern coast of Turkey, and the BBC World Service news reported that a fleet of some thirty Turkish warships - some carrying tanks, lorries and troops - had sailed for an unknown destination. A spontaneous hoot of ironic laughter went up at that. Unknown destination? You'd think at the very least they would have been able to hazard a guess.

The Turkish Cypriots now began to reinforce their local positions with heavy artillery. Things were hotting up. Across the field, at the back of the house, the familiar mound of Beehive Hill swarmed with uniformed Turkish Cypriots who dug in a machine-gun emplacement on the top. It looked like we might be going to get firing close at hand, and the thin walls of the pre-fabricated married quarters were made of asbestos. Harry turned the small study into a kind of war room. It had a large metal safe, set in bricks, which strengthened one wall and he propped a mattress up against the only window. A stout table was brought in and the children took up position on a pile of cushions underneath. Their job was to man the radio and tape-recorder and to ensure that no bulletins or instructions were missed. With a pair of binoculars we were able to peer over the top of the mattress and have a clear view of the Turkish Cypriot position on Beehive hill.

At dawn on Saturday the 20th of July 1974 the Turkish invasion of Cyprus began. The first landings were on the coast west of Kyrenia around the area of

Snake Island beach. Low flying aircraft dropped paratroops ahead of the seaborne divisions, which were backed up by phantoms of the Turkish air force. Turkish jets strafed the harbour at Kyrenia and a Greek Cypriot naval vessel was sunk. Fierce fighting broke out in the town and the surrounding villages, and innocent holiday-makers of a variety of nationalities found themselves trapped in their hotels. More paratroops were dropped into Turkish Cypriot-held areas around Nicosia and the advancing force was backed up by tanks. Nicosia airport and other key installations were bombed, and the island's broadcasting and telecommunications systems were taken over. Fighting later spread to Famagusta, and ahead of the invading army, the Greek Cypriot population fled south in fear of their lives.

As soon as the Turkish invasion began, the Commander British Forces Near East gave the order for all British military personnel and their dependents living in the Republic to be withdrawn into the safety of the Sovereign Bases. The sector warden plan was put into operation and convoys of cars and lorries formed up for the journey. Each family was allowed one small suitcase and no pets were permitted. Those living in married quarters on the bases now had to take in two or three other families. It was hoped that this would be a temporary measure for a few days only and then everyone would be able to return to their homes. It was decided to leave us in Berengaria as we were all together in an enclosed site. We were warned to stay indoors and listen for instructions on BFBS. During the morning there was a big explosion at the back of the house and a rattle of machine-gun fire. We took turns to keep watch with the binoculars over the top of the mattress and saw that the Greek Cypriots had set up a position to our right and were lobbing mortars at the Turkish Cypriots on Beehive Hill.

Several of Harry's RAF colleagues came in to see what was going on behind us and it got a bit crowded in the study as everyone watched the battle. A couple of British soldiers came by, checking that everyone was indoors. When they saw how near the firing was they immediately moved all the families on the outer perimeter into neighbours' houses further inside the enclave. Then the spoilsports fetched their major, who commandeered the quarter as an observation post and took over our war room! Heavy fighting had broken out again in Limassol, and somewhere around two o'clock, it was decided that the situation in Berengaria had become hazardous. We too were to be withdrawn into the bases.

12. WITHDRAWAL INTO THE BASES

It was the hottest day of the year and the heat was pretty unbearable as we formed up the convoy. Once all the houses had been checked and everyone had been accounted for, the long hot trek to safety began. It was a bit like being part of a waggon-train in the old wild west. Harry and some of his colleagues spaced themselves along the line of cars and, when the order came to set off, they encouraged them along like cowboy outriders on the trail.

"Ho - move 'em on out. Yip..."

The route to be taken was straight down from Berengaria to the Polemidia crossroads on the By-Pass, then right, via Kolossi and the M1, towards Akrotiri and Episkopi. The images of that evacuation remain vividly etched in my memory to this day. We were among the last to leave and a long line of vehicles stretched away down the road before us. Sporadic firing and explosions could be heard, and a thick column of black smoke was rising from the Turkish quarter below.

In these dangerous conditions several young women, many of them pushing prams and with toddlers in tow, were walking down the road. They were the wives of members of 1 Battalion Royal Scots Regiment - newly arrived on the island and living in hirings off the base. They did not know their way around and had no personal transport. Car doors were flung open and people crawling along in the convoy dived out, grabbing the young mothers and their children and hauling them into vehicles which had enough space.

Suddenly the sound of battle intensified and some UN soldiers directed the cars immediately in front of us across the *bundu.* They halted our car and indicated we should wait. Harry was driving, I had the camera at the ready in the passenger seat and the children manned the radio and tape recorder in the back. The sun beat relentlessly down, heating up the inside of the car.

When Greek and Turkish local factions began to engage on the *bundu,* the UN troops motioned to us to proceed in the original direction. We moved steadily down the empty road towards the crossroads, closely followed by one or two other cars carrying service families.

There were loud bursts of gunfire all round. and Harry briefed us on what to do as he inched cautiously along.

"When you hear that noise, Karen, you dive forward across the seat and you, Jeremy, you go across behind her. Sheila, you slide down below the level of the window."

"What about you, Daddy?" said Jeremy, always a thinker.

"Never you mind about..."

Harry didn't get a chance to finish. There was a huge burst of fire, and while we three sat there like idiots, he disappeared below the dashboard. All I could see of him were his two hands still clutching the steering wheel as we drove along. We took our telling-off with good grace and quickly learned to dive for cover after that.

We had almost reached the By-Pass when Harry had to stop so that we would not be caught in the cross-fire. On our left, some Turkish Cypriot soldiers were firing a machine-gun at some National Guardsmen on the right hand side, who had an old Gatling gun mounted on a lorry. We could see the Greek men clearly. The one in charge was the young husband of the locally employed clerk who worked at the Education Centre. He recognised Harry right away and held up his hand to warn him not to proceed. Then there came a lull in the firing as the Turks reloaded and he leapt forward, shouting and waving us on.

"OK sir, GO!"

He was heartbreakingly young, well-educated and a first class footballer. I prayed he would survive. My heart wept for him and all the others like him. What would become of our many Cypriot friends who, unlike us, had no place of sanctuary?

We reached the By-Pass to see two RAF policemen, unarmed and in shirt-sleeves, directing and controlling traffic through a hail of bullets. Their courage and fortitude under fire was exemplary, yet to look at them you would have thought they were directing traffic at Ascot on race day. We filtered into the column of vehicles travelling west. The terrified local population was fleeing the town. Those who had British passports would be able to enter the bases, but the majority would go to the mountains to hide.

The long line of cars moved a few metres and stopped. Children and babies were getting fractious and thirsty in the heat. We passed through Kolossi and eventually reached the M1 - the stretch of main road linking the Sovereign base areas of Akrotiri and Episkopi. Here the column divided - each family heading for the particular base at which the head of the family was stationed. We turned right towards Episkopi. At intervals along the road the Royal Scots, whose job it was to protect the bases, were positioned on tanks and armoured vehicles. Loud cheers came from the convoy as we passed their reassuring presence and grins of relief came over their faces as they recognised their wives and children in the cars.

There was another long hold-up at the far end of the M1. A fierce battle was raging in nearby Episkopi village. Loud explosions were accompanied by the rattle of automatic fire and a thick pall of black smoke was rising in the still air.

The hours passed. The temperature lowered slightly as evening fell and we had still not reached our destination. I stood beside the car above Curium beach, looking back towards Limassol, and my heart ached for the people and the tragedy that was befalling this lovely island.

At about a quarter past midnight we edged into the crowded car park at Episkopi. Volunteers were handing out tea. I dislike strong tea and do not take it with sugar, but the hot strong brew we sipped so thankfully that night tasted like nectar. Painfully slowly the cars left the car park for the families to be processed and accounted for by the desperately tired and overworked staff, who had been working non-stop for hours. When our turn came, there were only a hundred or so people left to accommodate. When we reached the desk we discovered that all available space in married quarters had been filled. It was time to improvise. The officer in charge looked up at Harry.

"You are the senior officer present. Commandeer a barrack block and get these people housed."

13. THE HAWKINS HOTEL

Large three-storey barrack blocks provided accommodation for single servicemen at Episkopi. The first one Harry approached was Block 3 which was occupied by young RAF policemen. Not only did they immediately volunteer to vacate the premises and sleep at their place of work, they also did everything they possibly could to help the desperately tired women and children to settle in. Somehow that night, with extra mattresses and pillows scrounged from various places, the last remaining evacuees were provided with somewhere to sleep. Harry was already logging people as they were allocated a space. The next morning there would follow a mammoth task of organisation.

At daybreak the noise was incredible. There were babies crying, children shouting and racing up and down three flights of tiled stairs, and a queue of people who all had something urgently requiring attention. The first had a complaint that every one of the lavatories was blocked with soiled nappies, reams of toilet paper and God knows what else. Harry called in the unblockers and turned to me.

"You will have to be in charge of hygiene. If that fails, morale will drop and life will be unbearable in here."

Many of the NCOs' wives were made of the stuff that made you proud to be British. I could not have coped without their support, their willingness to carry out any task, however ghastly, and above all their warmth and sense of humour.

Taking the worst cleaning job myself that morning, I organised a rota so that everyone shared in the daily swabbing and cleaning. Mindful of Harry's words, I insisted on a particularly high standard of cleanliness in the bathrooms and loos. Amongst other things, this served to earn me the name of Harpic Hawkins.

With the toilet facilities ship-shape again, it was time for breakfast. Unlike the people housed in married quarters, who were living on compo rations, our lucky residents had only a short walk across to the airmen's mess to be served three well-cooked meals a day.

Meanwhile Harry was busy organising with his deputy, the wonderful, invaluable Corporal Marsden. First of all they dragged a big counter across the middle of the entrance hall and set up on it telephones, radio, tape-recorder and a large notice which read 'HAWKINS HOTEL RECEPTION'. Instead of a register on the desk, a huge numbered chinograph sheet was attached to the wall. All one hundred and twenty residents were required to make note of their movements in and out of the block daily, so that everyone could be accounted for at all times.

An emergency generally tends to bring out the

best in people, and within minutes of making any kind of suggestion or request, someone would come up with an answer. Corporal Marsden knew his way around the base and had a very persuasive manner. There were no cots for the babies so he appropriated large strong packing cartons from stores. With the sides cut down and the bases lined with mattresses, which he recklessly cut to fit, they made excellent temporary cribs. There were not enough beds, so where there were several children together, spare mattresses were laid on the floor and they slept in rows. They loved it, of course, thinking it a great adventure. Each large room had to be shared by eighteen to twenty people, and to give them all as much privacy as possible, Harry and his right-hand man partitioned the rooms with cardboard boxes and rigged up heavy curtains. Only women and children were allowed in the block at night - the men going to their place of work to sleep.

Harry quickly realised there was a danger of possible friction with so many families, many of them complete strangers to each other, living cheek by jowl in crowded conditions at the hottest time of the year. It was vital that time should not pass slowly and aimlessly by. To this end he split the day up into segments.

Our block soon became the envy of many on the base. An hour after breakfast each day I was detailed to teach swimming again. Some landrovers would arrive, driven by RAF policemen who had life-saving qualifications. We then loaded up the children and took them to Paramali beach for a swimming lesson. Somewhere around eleven o'clock the infant and junior school teachers in the block made use of their skills by reading stories to the younger children, while the mothers got together for coffee and a chat. Lunch was followed by a mandatory siesta time. At six o'clock it was the turn of the teenagers, when a disco was set up in the hall and soft drinks were provided. At nine o'clock, with all children settled, the adults gathered in the reception area for Happy Hour. Here we could relax over a drink, air views, and make the most of the situation.

There was such a great atmosphere in our block that we never seemed to go short of anything, despite the cessation of normal deliveries to the base. Every now and then someone would pull up in a vehicle and drop off various hard-to-come-by goodies - cartons of crisps, packs of Coke, a box of fresh grapes or a few crates of beer.

"Found these lying around surplus to needs, sir. I'm sure you can make good use of them here..."

There was music, dancing and laughter. Hearts were won over and lasting friendships were formed in these most trying of circumstances. Morale was given a big boost early every morning as the band of the Royal Scots, instruments gleaming in the sunshine, marched through the camp. The rousing music and the sight of the bandsmen in their crisp khaki uniforms lifted our spirits as nothing else could, and we all stepped outside to applaud them as they marched past the block.

Instruments gleaming in the sunshine

Inevitably a huge strain was put on resources and manpower. Episkopi was bursting at the seams. Many Greek Cypriots who had British passports took shelter within the boundaries, and Turkish Cypriots from villages in the area now found themselves stranded in Greek-controlled territory. They fled to the base seeking sanctuary - walking over the hills in ones and twos. There were men, women and children of all ages. One four-year-old boy came in leading his blind grandmother by the hand. Most of the men carried weapons which they were relieved of before being allowed in. These refugees added an additional logistical problem on top of an already abnormal situation. Tented accommodation was set up in Happy Valley and they were temporarily housed in groups made up of their own village communities. Regular meals were provided and an appeal was launched for clothing. The sick and wounded were treated and all their immediate needs were catered for.

Extra nurses of the British armed forces were flown in and the station medical officers were kept extremely busy. Many of the Turks were wounded and in need of surgery, while there were numerous medical problems among the elderly. There were also several babies needing special care. The station medical centre at Episkopi, always busy at the best of times, now had an enormous workload with the huge influx of service families who would normally seek treatment at the large Service medical facility in Limassol. Conditions were crowded, and in the block we had to cope as far as possible with all relatively minor problems ourselves. I cannot speak too highly in praise of the Senior Medical Officer and his staff at the way they handled everything with such calm efficiency.

We had our share of sickness in the block. Chicken-pox broke out among the younger children and several people went down with a stomach ailment, colloquially referred to as the Troodos Trots. We segregated the sufferers where possible and nursed them as best we could, knowing we had expert help at the end of a telephone for anything serious.

From the time we arrived, the radio on the reception desk was manned at all times. It was from this that we were kept up to date with what was going on in the rest of the island. We were safely out of the firing line and had never felt ourselves to be in any real danger. Others, however, were not so lucky. We listened to the messages being broadcast to them.

"Famagusta Sector two. Keep your heads down and remain calm."

"To the people in Kyrenia. We have not forgotten you. We are doing our best to arrange your safe passage."

A massive operation was launched to rescue people trapped by the fighting in and around Kyrenia. Again, the radio was their only link with a safe way out of the war zone. The unflappable voice of the BFBS announcer calmly issued the vital information. Where possible, evacuees should make their way to the beaches east of Kyrenia, where ships of the British Royal Navy would be waiting offshore. Naval officers, recognisable by their white uniforms, would be ashore and their instructions were to be followed closely. So began a smooth, well-organised operation to lift people from the beaches by helicopter and transfer them to the waiting navy vessels.

Meanwhile, to the west of Kyrenia, those caught in the thick of the fighting had to endure three terrifying days and nights in the most dangerous of conditions. Eventually the Commander British Forces managed to arrange a five-hour cease-fire, and through broadcasts over the BFBS, the beleaguered and battle-weary people were instructed to make their way to the nearest beach and use white sheets to lay out a large letter H on the ground. Years later I met Susan MacDonald-Cacciotti, a features writer with 'The Times', who had been there at the time. She gave me an emotional first-hand account of her experience.

* * * * *

Susan was on holiday at a family home in Lapithos with her Italian husband and their two daughters - three-year-old Melissa and Luisa, just one year old. Accompanying them were the fifteen-year-old daughter from her husband's first marriage and an Iranian maid, who spoke only Farsi and had never before been outside Iran.

Susan's mother had also joined them for the holiday.

They had arrived on the island just before the coup. Like everyone else, they felt uncomfortable with the worsening situation and when a few days later fires began to burn all across the northern range of mountains, they became worried. The fires intensified, and seriously concerned now, they drove to Nicosia to seek advice. A representative of the British High Commission assured them there was no problem, but going on to visit Turkish friends in the city, they found them digging trenches in the garden. Their advice was to get out quickly!

The National Guard had announced that Nicosia airport was due to be opened within the next day or so and Susan's husband, the area manager for Alitalia based in Iran, arranged for an aircraft to be flown in specially to pick them up. On the morning of the planned departure they were up early doing the last minute packing when they heard aircraft overhead. This, they thought, was excellent news. The airport was obviously operational again. Then bombs began to fall all around them. The Alitalia plane would not be arriving after all, for the Turkish invasion of Cyprus had begun.

Shells from the Greek Cypriot positions in the hills above Lapithos began to whine overhead as the Turkish navy pounded the Kyrenia mountains from the sea and landing craft brought the invasion troops ashore. Meanwhile, low flying aircraft dropped paratroops ahead of the main force.

Fires began to rage out of control in the tinder-dry area surrounding the house. They were in an unenviable and extremely hazardous position - the lovely old village house afforded little protection from the concentrated onslaught. Below them on the coast was a newly-built hotel, and feeling that they might be safer in a building made of reinforced concrete, they telephoned the manager and asked whether he thought it would be a good idea for them to move down. He told them to stay where they were - the Turks were landing on the hotel beach.

Their worries increased when an old World War Two cannon was dragged into position against the back gate. Then the telephone rang. It was the manager from the hotel saying that there appeared to be a lull in the landings and the Turkish troops were now moving towards Lapithos. They should make an immediate attempt to get down to the coast. Piling into the hired car, they sped down the tortuous, twisting road towards the hotel. They did not meet the invasion force on the way down, and miraculously they were not hit by bombs or shellfire. Nor did they plunge off the mountainside in their hasty descent.

When they reached the hotel it was to find some hundred people of different nationalities huddled in the basement in a state of shock. There they spent the night, while the firing and shelling outside continued unabated. The manager and the chef, both Greek Cypriots, stayed with them and did everything they could to make the guests more comfortable. Mattresses were brought down from the bedrooms, but no one slept.

The next morning brought some even worse news. BFBS radio reported that the Turks believed that holiday hotels along the coast were being used by Greek Cypriot fighters. They advised people trapped in these hotels to raise their own national flags, but there was no way anyone could make an attempt to do so at that point. Non-stop firing continued throughout the morning. Then, at lunchtime, their place of refuge suddenly shuddered under a large impact. Realising they had been hit, Susan told me she came to understand the meaning of feeling sick with fear. Some people were actually physically sick with terror. The manager and the chef dashed upstairs to see what had happened. They returned with the news that a hole had been blown in a wall, some four floors up, leaving the rooms covered with building debris and broken glass.

The Turkish navy gunners quickly found their range and, shortly afterwards, the hotel took a direct hit. The building began to burn fiercely and was soon engulfed in thick, black, toxic smoke. The basement caved in but by a strange quirk of fate, (some might say by the hand of God) as one side turned to rubble, the other side blew out and they were left with an exit through which they could clamber on to the sharp volcanic rocks outside.

In remembering, Susan told me she could not speak too highly of the hotel manager and the chef who stayed with them. The chef, a giant of a man, lined them up and ordered them out of the burning building into the hazardous conditions outside. He did not mince words. He spoke sharply to those reluctant to move.

"If you stay here, you die."

Outside there was no shelter from the intense firing, but they took cover as best they could in the hollows formed by the sea among the rocks. During a brief lull in the fighting, the two Cypriots again risked their lives by returning to the hotel to bring the last of the drinking water in two large buckets. They conserved it by strict rationing, allowing a little more each time for the children.

In this exposed position they stayed, without food, for three days and three nights, while the battle raged around them and the surrounding villages and fields went up in flames. Fortunately, the Iranian maid had hung on to a bag containing baby food and nappies, so the smallest member of the party was fed and changed throughout the ordeal.

Susan's father was Alistair MacDonald, son of the former British Prime Minister, Ramsay MacDonald. He had originally designed the British Sovereign Bases on the island, and from her knowledge of the bases, she realised that their only hope of rescue would come through the British Forces. She insisted on the importance of tuning the radio to BFBS and listening at all times. In the event, her insistence on this point proved to be the source of their salvation.

The Commander British Forces eventually managed to arrange a five-hour cease-fire, and one of the British naval frigates accompanying HMS Hermes came close inshore. White sheets in the form of a letter H were laid out on the rocks as instructed and soon people were being taken from the beaches by helicopter and a flotilla of small boats. In the confusion the family became separated. Along with many others, Susan's husband was plucked from the rocks by helicopter and lifted across to the waiting ship. Susan found herself in a small boat being rowed by, amongst others, the hotel manager. They were among the last to be picked up - shelling had already resumed as they pushed off from the beach.

No one was asked for proof of nationality. In these extreme circumstances, the saving of human life was paramount. The chef stayed with his guests until he saw that they were safe. Then, turning his back on his own safety, he set off inland to join up with the Greek fighting force.

They spent the first night on board the frigate. Looking back towards the shore, it seemed to Susan that the whole island was on fire, with a thick pall of black smoke rising in the air. Some refugees needed medical attention. Many were completely traumatised by the terrifying experience they had undergone and the terrible scenes they had witnessed. Other hotels further along the coast had been attacked and the Greek Cypriot staff lined up and shot by the invading troops in front of the horrified tourists. Susan was later to learn that their hotel was the only one along that stretch of coast that Turkish troops did not enter. Seeing it had received a direct hit and was burning so fiercely, they had assumed that no one in there could have been left alive.

Those needing treatment were transferred immediately to the sick-bay on HMS Hermes. Meanwhile, the navy had a lot of starving people on their hands. The ship's cooks opened every tin of meat and vegetables they could lay their hands on, throwing the contents with abandon into a glorious impromptu stew to give the evacuees their first taste of food in three days. Unorthodox it might have been. The diners' verdict? Delicious.

The following morning, after breakfast, all the refugees were transferred to the aircraft carrier. They were taken below the flight deck and sat in long rows while trestle tables were set up and the inevitable task of processing and identifying everyone began. When they came to Susan's family they did a double-take. Susan, her mother and the two little girls all had British passports. Her husband's was Italian. His daughter, by his first marriage, travelled with an American passport and the maid's was Iranian.

A short sea-voyage around the coast to Akrotiri, courtesy of the Royal Navy, and a long-haul flight to the UK on a Hercules transport, courtesy of the Royal Air Force, finally brought their ordeal to an end.

Because of the severity of the traumatic conditions they had endured, they were flown out of Akrotiri within an hour of their arrival on HMS Hermes - leap-frogging the hundreds of people still waiting there to go.

* * * * *

The Commander of the British Forces had personally broadcast a message to the Greek and Turkish commanders in the area, telling them that, as with the convoys that had previously been organised, this was a purely humanitarian operation. It was intended to save the lives of innocent people who, through no fault of their own, found themselves caught up in the fighting. He reminded them that the Union Jack was instantly recognisable and that his men had orders not to fire unless in self defence. In the event, the Turks watched the evacuation carefully but took no action to hinder or impede its progress. In Block 3 we all agreed it was a wise decision on their part not to mess with the Royal Navy and the RAF.

Paphos, with the enclaved Turkish quarter of Moutoullas, had been taking a pounding. The town was a Makarios stronghold and had already been singled out for a concentrated attack by the National Guard during the coup. Now the Turks shelled it from the sea and, to everyone's amusement and Greek delight, they managed to sink one of their own ships.

Most foreigners living in Paphos had already

left in a United Nations convoy. Later, when things really began to hot up, those remaining in the town were also advised to leave. Among them was a charming lady who subsequently took refuge in our block. Her name was Peggy O'Neill. In 1971 she and her husband had established a successful confectionery, cake and coffee house in the centre of the town. When her husband died, soon afterwards, this lovely Irishwoman continued to run it on her own with style and humour.

The UN peace-keeping force on the island had an Irish contingent of three hundred troops stationed nearby at St. Patrick's camp on the Paphos-Polis road. Her establishment, affectionately known as Peggy's, became the regular off-duty meeting place for the Irish soldiers. She listened to their troubles and made them feel at home. She reproved them when they became too boisterous and saw they were safely returned to camp when they became too drunk.

Peggy stayed to keep the business running when the first evacuation of foreign nationals took place, but as the situation worsened, she heeded the advice of the UN commander and was brought out under fire, in the last convoy out of Paphos, huddled in the back of a lorry driven by her Irish boys. Unharmed but badly shaken by the experience, she immediately asked what she could do to help. Her gentle caring manner was an inspiration and we have remained lifelong friends.

During the crisis, we had been wondering what would happen to our new car. Under normal circumstances it would have been shipped back to the UK, for we had only a few more weeks of our three-year tour left. There was a distinct possibility that it might have to be abandoned. Then came a telephone call from an RAF sergeant whom Harry knew well. He was working on the airfield at Akrotiri and said that big transport aircraft, carrying military equipment needed for the protection of the bases, were being unloaded, turned round in record time, and sent back practically empty.

"If you can get the car over here, sir, with the necessary paperwork, I'll get it loaded on."

This was too good a chance to miss.

"There's no way I can leave," said Harry. "You'll have to do it. Get the forms filled in and look out for Russ on the airfield. Once you find him he'll do the rest."

It wasn't quite as simple as it seemed. With a big Union Jack flying from the passenger window and the other windows covered in stickers, I set off for Akrotiri. The Royal Marines had set up check-points at intervals along the route and the Royal Scots were in evidence in their tanks and armoured cars. I was stopped at the first point and a young marine looked at my passport. He saw my place of birth as being Torquay and beamed, speaking in a broad Devonshire accent.

"Oh, you're one of us, are you love?"

He too had been born in Torquay and was stationed at Seaton Barracks in Devon. He rang ahead to the next check point.

"There's a *janner* coming through, lads, and she's in a hurry."

Thereafter I sailed through without stopping, receiving cheery waves from my compatriots on the way. Once through the gate at Akrotiri I made my way down to the main dispersal area. An incredible sight met my eyes. It was the first time I had seen the RAF base on a war footing and it is something I shall never forget. Hundreds of airmen and soldiers, stripped to the waist, were swarming like ants over the airfield. Under the intense heat of the August sun, they were unloading incoming flights and turning them round, in the space of forty minutes, ready for take-off. Tanks and helicopters were emerging from the darkened interiors of huge transport aircraft, together with military vehicles and large crates of spare parts. The noise was deafening as engines were turned over. Big transports taxied on the runway and helicopters whirled overhead.

I parked the car and stood looking down at the heaving dispersal pans, wondering how on earth I was going to find my contact in the midst of all the organised chaos. Then I heard a piercing whistle, followed by my name, and there was Russ, standing on top of a tank, waving both arms to attract my attention. I made my way down to him and he pointed out the building where I was to take the paperwork for approval. Once I had done that, I was to leave it in the car with the keys in the ignition and he would do his best to get it loaded on.

An hour later, with one final wave, I set off to hitch-hike my way back. I hadn't even reached the main gate before some Royal Marines rescued me. On their way to Episkopi, they hauled me up into their landrover and, seemingly breaking the world land speed record, dropped me off outside Block 3 in next to no time.

Once the rescued holiday-makers and foreign nationals had been flown out of Akrotiri by the Royal Air Force, other categories were sent back to the UK. Pregnant women and those with medical or psychological problems were evacuated as soon as possible. Then, as and when aircraft became available, they began to call forward the families of personnel who had less than a month or two still left to serve on the island.

Ten days after the Turkish invasion, late at night a flight list marked 'urgent' appeared on the reception desk. A VC10 was leaving in the early hours of the morning carrying evacuees back to England. Harry scanned the list then looked up and met my eye. The children and I had one hour's notice to leave Cyprus for good.

14. UK-BOUND

Tears rolled down my face as the VC10 taxied through the dawn sea-mist shrouding the runway. As if in sympathy, slow droplets of water rolled down the outside of the small circular window as I looked out on Akrotiri for the last time. My young son, sensing my sadness, slid his hand in mine. My thirteen-year-old daughter, Karen, tossed her blonde hair, tightened her seatbelt and smiled at me. How grown-up and self-assured she seemed to me now. Where several mature women had come apart at the seams under the strain, she had risen to meet the challenge.

Freed of pressing responsibilities for the time being, my mind wandered back over the events of the past few weeks. I wondered how the desperately worried English girl from Oxford was faring. She had arrived at our block, with her seven-week-old baby, not knowing where her young Greek Cypriot husband was - or even whether he was alive or dead. She could not go back to Limassol because of the fighting, and when she told me her mother lived in Oxford, Harry made arrangements for her to be flown out as soon as possible. Realising there was really no other option, she went to complete the essential paperwork, leaving her baby asleep in a carrycot behind the desk in the reception area.

Before long, the child woke and began to cry. Seeing I was tied up with a crowd of anxious women and children, Karen, herself little more than a child, calmly picked the infant up and soothed it. I still have a vivid recollection of her, amid the noise and confusion, sitting quietly nursing the tiny baby while several small children sat around her feet gazing raptly up at her as she told them a story.

I thought of the British wives of prominent Greek Cypriot business men and doctors who had taken refuge in the Hawkins Hotel. Their normal lifestyle could not have been further from the conditions in which we found ourselves, but grateful for the safe haven, they did everything they could to help and comfort others, and willingly took their turn at the most rotten cleaning jobs.

I hoped someone would remember to scrounge some scraps from the kitchen for Black Mak coup de cat. A tiny soot-black kitten with emerald eyes, he had appeared at the block on the day we moved in and immediately made himself at home. We adopted him as our mascot and he was a great favourite with everyone.

What had become of Safia and her children? Were they safely enclaved somewhere - or had they perished in the fighting? There had been no time for goodbyes. We had all suddenly been wrenched from our homes, leaving all our belongings behind. As we headed westward and home, we had only the light clothing we were wearing and some clean underwear and T-shirts in a small grip.

The runway at Brize Norton was not operational on the day we flew in, so the aircraft touched down at RAF Fairford in Gloucestershire. We shivered as we stepped out into the cool English summer breeze. Buses were waiting to take us for processing at Brize and the children were delighted to see a tall red double-decker among them. Of course there was nothing for it but to ride upstairs. Oh well, we didn't have any luggage anyway. So up we went. As the bus drove along a narrow country road, an overhanging branch dragged along the side of the upstairs windows with a sound like machine-gun fire. Everyone on the bus except the driver hit the floor, so thoroughly had we become conditioned.

Everything that could possibly be done to help us was done. I was asked whether I needed accommodation anywhere and when I replied that we would go to my mother in Plymouth, a railway warrant was immediately made out and we were allocated space in the next vehicle to leave for Swindon railway station. The Red Cross provided us with sweaters for the journey and, almost before we knew it, we were gazing upon the lush green fields of Devon once more. It was with mixed feelings that I stepped from the train, my mind almost numb with fatigue. Reassuring to be swept up in my brother's big bear-hug as we stood on the platform and comforting to see my mother, with outstretched arms and tears of relief running down her face, as the children dashed down the drive of her home in Plymstock. But my thoughts returned again and again to Harry, left behind to get on with running the Hawkins Hotel without me.

The next morning there was a piece of incredibly good news to lift our spirits. I received a telephone call from a garage in Carterton, Oxfordshire. They had taken delivery of a Saab 99 in my name. Would I like them to deliver it to Plymstock the following day? It was good to have our own transport. We went into Plymouth to buy new clothes and return our refugee sweaters to the Red Cross. I had brought back several rolls of film with me which were in for developing and which I was eager to see. When we went to pick them up, my mother indicated a nearby restaurant which, she said, served an excellent cup of coffee. She suggested we rest awhile and look at the photographs.

We ordered our drinks and passed the photos around. Some were of the coup and the evacuation following the invasion, but others had been taken in the Kyrenia area a few days before the outbreak of hostilities. A lady brought the coffee over to us. I had heard her speaking in Greek behind the counter, and without even thinking I thanked her in the same language. It provoked an amazing response. She and her husband, together with another couple, crowded around our table, all asking questions at once. They were Greek

Cypriots and wanted to know if I had just returned from the island. What news did I have? Did I know what had happened to the people in the villages surrounding Kyrenia? I had no words of comfort for them. If they had been watching television news bulletins, they probably knew more about what had been going on in the northern part of Cyprus than I did. Two of the people were relatives of the restaurant owners. They came from Ayios Georgios, just west of Kyrenia, and were in England for a two-week holiday. They were worried about their father, an old man who lived in Bellapais. Did I know what had happened to the Greek Cypriot men from that village?

All I had was the recent photographs. I handed them to the man from Ayios Georgios. He leafed through them until, suddenly, he came upon one Harry had taken of a group of old men sitting beneath the Tree of Idleness. He gazed at it, then bowed his head and wept, wordlessly passing the photograph to his wife. The remaining family members scrutinised the picture and they all became extremely emotional. When they recovered somewhat, it was to tell me that one of the men sitting under the tree was their father. There had been no news of him since the Turks invaded and they feared the worst.

Their annual holiday in the UK was being forcibly extended, causing great inconvenience all round. Now they lovingly described the familiar places they recognised in the pictures. They were impatient to

Beneath the Tree of Idleness

get back to find out at first hand what had happened. They wanted to find their father and then get on with their lives. I gave them the photographs of Bellapais and, feeling somewhat downcast by the encounter, we made our way home.

In the years to come, I was often to think of this particular family, whose lives had briefly touched mine. For, despite their fear that it would take time, they could not know that they would never be able to return to their homes.

My own father had died some years earlier. Now, grateful to have my mother safe and well, we continued to enjoy our holiday in Devon and wait for Harry's return to the UK.

Meanwhile in Cyprus, on the first of August, just a day or so after our sudden flight out, the situation in Limassol was deemed safe enough for families to be allowed back to their homes. All kinds of horror stories were reported - from shell holes in walls and bullet holes in doors, to bloodstained bedding and dead dogs in the garden. The electricity supply had been cut and food had rotted in fridges and freezers. Houses had been broken into by combatants seeking shelter and many places had suffered considerable damage. Homes were cleaned up, larders re-stocked and Service families slowly began to pick up the threads of their lives.

It was too good to last. Two weeks later the peace talks in Geneva came to an abrupt end and the Turkish army continued its advance southwards. They now occupied a line from east to west roughly across the middle of the island - effectively sealing off the north. Once again, British families were withdrawn into the bases. The following day the decision was taken to return to the UK all the families of personnel who did not live in married quarters within the Sovereign Base Areas. A massive airlift was mounted and wives found themselves flying out at less than an hour's notice with no time to say goodbye to their husbands. Many had no idea where they would be taken on arrival. Those who had nowhere to go were allocated accommodation, as far as possible, in an area nearest to their choice. In many cases it was several days before heads of families had any idea where their wives and children had been settled.

A few days later, another impressive operation was mounted. This time to recover an estimated four million pounds worth of personal belongings that had been left behind in Limassol. We had all been allowed one small suitcase when we left, and everything else we owned was still in our homes. It was a daunting task, but with the usual smooth organisation shown by the British Forces and with the co-operation of the authorities now controlling the Republic, operation code name 'Snatch' was a resounding success.

During this period, Harry was able to return to Berengaria to try and save as much of our stuff as he could in the time available. He says he remembers mostly how lonely and empty the house looked, and how deserted the normally lively little enclave appeared. The only sound was that of hammering and nailing as everyone worked with a will to crate up their belongings.

How lucky we were, though. We had never felt ourselves to be in any real danger. What of the Cypriots who had lost their lives and the many more who were still missing? All Greek Cypriots who lived north of the Green Line dividing the island lost their homes and everything else they owned - land that had been in their family for generations, their orchards, livestock, and their businesses. Those who did not flee found themselves in the unbelievable position of being refugees in their own country. No one really believed it was a situation that could last for long. After all, there were three Guarantor Powers and the UN itself was closely involved. Was not a situation such as this, one of the very reasons the UN had been formed in the first place?

Harry's tour of duty in Cyprus ended within a few weeks and he too returned to England. The children and I were at the airport to meet him, and from there we drove straight to Nottinghamshire to see where we would be living for the next three years. He was to join the staff of the Royal Air Force School of Education at Newton.

15. WHERE ARE YOU NOW, CRAIG?

We moved into a married quarter at Syerston, an old disused airfield about ten miles or so away from the School of Education. It was a fairly isolated windswept place, and that winter we felt the cold as we had never done before. Thick snow covered the ground, and the east wind numbed our fingers and faces no matter how well we wrapped ourselves up when we went out. Freezing fog and black ice made road conditions treacherous. We always seemed to be travelling up and down the A46 for one reason or the other - Harry to work, the children to school, and me to a big Sports Centre to teach swimming in the evenings.

With no chance of moving into a quarter on the base itself and determined not to spend another winter sliding up and down the old Fosse Way, we somehow scraped up enough money to put a deposit on a house. It proved to be one of the smartest moves we ever made. We bought the house, complete with curtains and fitted carpets, in the small village of Bingham and willingly slept on mattresses on the floor until we managed to get the place properly furnished. It was warm and cosy and, most importantly, central to where we wanted to be.

We have many happy memories of the time we spent there. I missed Cyprus and the laid-back way of life, but the busy days flew by as we settled into our new home and gradually became part of the small community. Bingham had a big modern Sports Centre and I had a full teaching schedule with classes for adult non-swimmers. All my students came with one thing in common - they were all utterly terrified of the water. Affordable package tours to Spain were in their heyday, and people who had previously never thought it necessary to learn to swim now considered swimming lessons a priority. They had begun to realise just how much they were missing by not being able to cool off in the hotel swimming pool when they took their hard-earned holidays abroad.

I had the ideal teaching pool. It was roomy and beautifully warm, even in the depths of winter. It was also only a few feet deep, and because it was built mainly above ground level, I was able to walk all around the sides and keep contact with my pupils. Whatever the reasons put forward by non-swimmers for their predicament - and there are a variety of those - the basic cause is the same in each case. It is quite simply fear. Swimming is all about confidence. The reason people think they cannot swim is because they are afraid. The fact is they can all swim. The secret of success is getting them to believe it. Throw an animal in the water and it will immediately start to swim, even though it may never have seen an expanse of water in its life. Self-preservation will make it use its limbs to propel itself to safety. Human beings do not react instinctively in the same way. They are more likely to throw their arms in the air and shout for help as they go down - which they surely will if they try to walk on water.

It was nothing less than amazing to see just how quickly most people would start to swim, once they understood the fundamental truth and overcame their fear. The specific gravity of water being greater than that of homo sapiens did the rest. All I did was give them the confidence they needed. I always tried to do this with understanding and a great deal of humour. Once they were waterborne, we could then progress to the techniques of the various strokes. Their pride and delight in their success made it one of the most rewarding teaching jobs I ever had. I was very well paid for my efforts, but the job satisfaction far outweighed the financial reward.

One incident from that era remains for ever etched in my memory. I had driven across to another Nottinghamshire town to take a look at a newer more modern swimming pool that had just opened. It boasted all kinds of new-fangled ideas and an unusual layout. My children, of course, couldn't wait to try out the new facilities and were soon sliding down chutes and investigating the varied aspects of the pool. I was sitting in the cafeteria with the centre's swimming coach when I saw a young lifeguard leap over the guard-rail and dive in.

An alarm bell began to clang and we dashed out to see a small boy being pulled, unconscious, from the water. He was not breathing, and my companion immediately began mouth to mouth resuscitation. The child did not respond and it was fairly clear that he had suffered a cardiac arrest. I jumped down beside the little boy and felt for the carotid artery in his neck. There was no pulse and he was rapidly turning blue. No one knew how long he had been at the bottom of the pool.

Thankful for the time I had spent practising on Slack Alice, the resuscitation dummy, and mindful that you can all too easily break a child's ribs in attempting to restore a heartbeat, I sent up a silent prayer for help and began external cardiac massage combined with mouth to mouth. The prayer was answered. There was a visible response after the fifth set of compressions, and by the time the ambulance arrived he was crying loudly and gulping in lovely great lungfuls of air.

The following day, Harry received a telephone call from a Senior Aircraftsman at RAF Newton. He wanted to offer thanks and let us know that his six-year-old son, having been kept in hospital overnight for observation, had just been released none the worse for his ordeal. There was no brain damage and he had sustained no serious injury. That small blond boy must now be twenty-five years old. I often think of you, Craig Mooney, and wonder how you are.

* * * * *

Harry stayed at the School of Education for four years. It was a long time for us to stay in one place. Inevitably, however, a new posting came through. We were to go to Hereford. Harry was appointed Training Control Officer at the RAF Training School at Credenhill. The surrounding countryside was beautiful after the rather flat landscape we had experienced in Lincolnshire and Nottinghamshire. The Wye valley was picturesque and the Brecon Beacons within easy driving distance.

We sold our home in Bingham and bought a house overlooking the grounds of the Hereford Rugby Club. Karen, who was seventeen by then, was training at a secretarial college and would soon be off to London to work in Whitehall. With Harry at work and Jeremy at school, I needed something to keep me occupied. Unfortunately, there was no sports centre in Hereford. The building that housed the Hereford Swimming Baths, however, was being extended. Squash courts, a gym and a sauna were among other facilities to be offered, and a new young manager had been appointed by the town council to get it all going.

I went to see him and he gave me a tour of the new-look centre. It was sited in a lovely park alongside the river Wye. There was plenty of room and I estimated that a variety of classes, which had never been offered up until now, would be easy to set up. The manager had a budget to stick to, however, and was a little wary of overstepping the mark. In addition he was not too certain how these new ideas might be received.

"OK," I said. "I'll set up some classes and work for a month for nothing. If they take off and start making money, you can put me on the payroll. If they bomb, you won't have lost anything."

We shook hands on the deal, and before long I had yoga relaxation sessions going alongside more vigorous exercise classes. A slimming club, where we combined a weigh-in each week with alternating work-outs in the gym and the pool followed by a session in the sauna, was tremendously popular. Sometimes I took my little clan into the park for a walk or to play team games like rounders. I had a variety of swimming classes - from private schools to a special school for deaf children. I loved that work. All it took was to get the children to use their eyes while I used exaggerated mime. They were bright little souls, and once they knew what was expected of them they were quick to learn. And how they loved the freedom they experienced in the water.

I now wished I still had the little Isetta to get me to work. We continually had to make arrangements to cover various commitments when we both needed the car at the same time. Then Harry went up several notches in my estimation. He said we would have to get me a car of my own. A week or so later he bought me an Austin Healey Sprite. This magnificent two-seater sports car was in beautiful condition with gleaming bodywork and leather upholstery, both finished in black.

I felt like a million dollars driving the little gem with its throaty purr. Jeremy couldn't wait to get his hands on it. Not yet old enough to have a licence, he learned to drive it on the big empty car park of the Hereford Town Football Club when there were no matches being played.

Later that year the Amateur Swimming Association, sponsored by Cadburys Chocolate, selected a few pools in the UK, with resident ASA-qualified teachers, to set up mother and baby swimming classes. Ours was one of those chosen and I had babies from only a few weeks old in the warm water. It was a lot of fun and the sessions were nearly always oversubscribed.

One morning the boss came and warned us that the following day we should be smartly attired and on our best behaviour. National television cameras would be on the premises to interview him about the mother and baby classes, which had been attracting a lot of attention. For us the next day was business as usual. The pool staff always looked smart in their white singlets anyway, and I wore a T-shirt with the Cadbury logo displayed, which had been provided by the ASA. The boss, normally rather casually dressed, rolled up in a suit and tie!

The TV crew arrived and began to set up their equipment. The programme was called Today and the regional presenter was a big man called Alan Towers, with an extremely professional manner and a great sense of humour. He asked a few pertinent questions, and when the boss enquired where he should stand, he looked towards me and replied matter of factly.

"Well, she's the teacher, I'll do the interview with her."

To say there was a stunned silence would be an understatement. Then my colleagues were all falling about laughing in the background - as much at the boss's discomfiture as at the thought of me suddenly having to appear on national television. I must have looked pretty desperate, for Alan came over and sat beside me on the edge of the pool. He quietly asked me a few questions about the class and, when I protested that I had no idea how to go about a TV interview, calmly replied that we would simply be chatting exactly as we were doing now. I was to ignore the cameras and concentrate on him. There was nothing to it. First of all, though, they were going to film an introduction for the item.

Never believe all you see on TV. Alan changed into a pair of swimming trunks and stood on the edge of the teaching pool. He did a rapid spiel and said he was there to join the class for a session. Then, as the camera rolled, he crammed his arms through a brightly coloured and very small rubber ring and jumped into the water with a huge splash. It was so shallow it barely reached his waist. He then took a deep breath and lay on the bottom of the pool - re-emerging after a few seconds with an upwards thrust and arms raised over his head. When this was edited and shown later that night, it looked for all the world as if he had jumped into a deep pool and come right up again.

He dried himself off and at last we were ready. At least he was. I was still panic-stricken and totally unprepared. He did his best to put me at ease, then, being an inveterate joker, just before the red light came on he said conversationally: "Don't worry, Sheila, there are only three and a half million people watching you."

God alone knows how I got through the next ten minutes or whatever it was. Half of me was petrified and the other half wanted to laugh. I was conscious that everyone who worked at the centre was up in the seating area behind the cameras watching the proceedings. Fortunately, the bright lights prevented me from seeing their faces - for there were several jokers among that lot too.

Just eighteen months into the Hereford tour, Harry came home early one day. I could see something was up - he was bursting to give me some news and, from the expression on his face, it was obviously good.

"My desk officer rang me today. He wants to know if I'd mind being short-toured and posted overseas as Senior Education and Training Officer."

"Where?"

"RAF Akrotiri, Cyprus."

16. RETURN TO CYPRUS

In August, exactly six years after I had left the island in tears, I stepped out once more into the brilliant sunshine and shimmering heat of Akrotiri. In an instant it was as though I had never been away. The breeze carried the familiar unmistakable smell of sun-dried herbs, so evocative of Cyprus, and the searing heat bounced up off the tarmac. Harry, who had flown out a few weeks earlier, waved from the terrace of the air terminal building. He had found a hiring in Limassol where we would live for a couple of months while we waited for the married quarter we had been allocated to become available. The Education Centre was large, and among other specifications on his terms of reference, Harry was the Senior Counsellor for the Open University in Cyprus. This time we would be required to live at Akrotiri.

Our temporary home was a brand new house situated on the outskirts of town on the side nearest the Sovereign Bases. I enjoyed the couple of months that we lived there. I was free to visit old friends and re-explore Limassol. I found it greatly changed. Many more buildings had gone up - including tall blocks of flats which altered the whole appearance of the town. Tourism was beginning to take off again, and more and more hotels and apartments were being constructed.

The British flavour of the town had disappeared with the exodus of Service families during the invasion. The once crowded area previously known as Little London was no more. The NAAFI, Sick Quarters and the Island Club did not exist. On the By-Pass the Adult Education Centre and Unicorn House, once key British Forces institutions, had been converted to other purposes by their Cypriot owners. Signs and advertising hoardings which used to be mainly in English now proclaimed their messages in Greek. As the years passed, other languages would become prominent, firstly German and Arabic, then, later still, Russian.

Many refugees were still housed in tented accommodation, which was gradually being replaced by permanent buildings. Others were living in houses belonging to Turks who had moved north in 1974.

Almost before I realised, it was time to move to Akrotiri. Harry had taken over a large detached house with a big garden in a quiet cul-de-sac. By strange coincidence, it was right opposite the house Josie and Bill had occupied on our earlier tour. The rooms were large and airy, and the bedroom verandahs overlooked the blue Mediterranean. Once again I inherited a batwoman - this time a Greek Cypriot. She was from Ayios Mammas village and her name was Skevoulla.

Skevoulla spoke little English when we first met, and was delighted that we could more or less converse in Greek - although my forays into that language were pretty pathetic. Always cheerful, she was an extremely hard worker and kept me in order for three years. She was unmarried, and longed for a husband, children and a home of her own.

The Education Centre boasted a large hall and it was here that I soon found myself once again teaching exercise classes. A mixture of yoga relaxation, stretches and aerobics, the course was listed as Body Toners and we had T-shirts which proclaimed this on the front. It was the era when T-shirts with a message were the norm. My favourite was 48 Command engineering workshops which read 'U bend 'em, we mend 'em'. There were some which stated 'Glider pilots do it quietly' and 'Water skiers do it standing up'. Ours had an outline of someone in a leotard and 'Body Toners do it beautifully'. Dozens of women enrolled, and we held several sessions a week. We had a lot of fun as well as getting a good workout. Sometimes we did aerobics in formation. One day Harry happened to be showing the visiting Red Arrows aerobatic team around the Centre while we were in action.

"We're good at formation work," they said.

They pulled on some of the spare T-shirts and joined enthusiastically in the class. When we finished, most of the girls requested their autographs and it was very enlightening to see what they came up with for them to sign.

We often had visiting VIPs at the Centre, and while Harry did the official bit with the big chief, I was sometimes detailed to show his lady around. A Group

Captain from Strike Command came once, accompanied by his wife. The Centre was spick and span and Harry had cautioned Khan, a slightly built and very polite Asian who served cold drinks to the students, that a very important person would be arriving. Khan spoke little or no English.

"Yes sir," he replied.

He was never sure how to address me but, as I was the wife of a 'sir', he always called me sir as well.

When the big moment came, I was the first to walk past his drinks stall with the Group Captain's wife. I introduced him to her.

"This is Khan, who provides us with an excellent and essential service. Good morning, Khan."

"Good morning, sir." he said to me. Then, as she also greeted him, he looked frantically at me and back at her again. He realised she was a Group Captain's wife and therefore more important than me, but he had no idea how to acknowledge this. Then he had a flash of inspiration. He smiled broadly at the lady and lobbed in an extra one.

"Good morning, sir sir," he said.

Christmas drew near and there were endless squadron parties and get-togethers. The Christmas Draw in the Mess was a formal event with men in dinner jackets and ladies in long evening dress. In contrast the attire for New Year's Eve was Fancy Dress. Everyone let their hair down at this event, and there were some weird and wonderful costumes. Harry once went in full Arab dress complete with a false nose and moustache. No one had any idea who it was until we sat down for dinner together and he had to take his moustache off to eat.

Soon after Christmas my plans went somewhat awry. I had to go into the RAF hospital for surgery. A month or so later I was in there again for a second lot. Usually as fit as a flea, I came out feeling as though I had been run over by a bus. I was ordered to take things easy for a couple of months. Skevoulla was an absolute gem. She fussed over me like a mother hen and I wasn't allowed to lift a finger in the house.

A week or so after I got out of hospital came the worst day of my life. The telephone rang early on Easter Sunday morning. It was my brother to tell me my mother had died during the night. My mind went numb - I was unable to speak. The shock almost floored me. She had not been ill, and in another ten days she would have been flying out to Cyprus to stay with us.

There were no flights out of Akrotiri because it was Easter, so I was driven by service car to Larnaca and taken directly on board a Cyprus Airways flight to Heathrow. Once we were airborne, the pilot spoke over the intercom.

"Would Mrs Hawkins please make herself known to the cabin staff."

They were kindness itself and I will never forget it. I was looked after at every step of the journey. It was snowing at Swindon railway station when I spoke on the phone to a corporal who was due to meet me.

"How will I know you, Ma'am?" he asked.

"That's easy, Corporal," I said. "I'll be the only idiot standing on the platform in a snowstorm wearing summer sandals and a white pleated skirt."

Somehow my brother and I got through the awful days that followed. The day after the funeral dawned clear and sunny, although the wind was cold. The next day I would be returning to Cyprus. We went to the little village of Newton Ferrers to have lunch at a favourite pub by the river. I walked through the lovely country lanes looking at the rich, red Devon earth and inhaling the fragrance of the Devon violets my mother had loved so much. Pale primroses bloomed on the roadside bank and a song thrush sang from a bough above our heads. Painted boats bobbed idly on the water. On a slipway, one man was painting the keel of his upturned rowing boat. Everything seemed unnaturally clear and bright, yet in some strange way I felt as if I no longer belonged. It was the end of an era.

* * * * *

As the VC10 let down over the familiar terrain at Akrotiri, I felt as though I was truly home. The family ties which had anchored me to Devon since my childhood were severed with the death of my mother. I recovered well from the surgery while I grieved for her. When I went back to work, it was to keep to a less

I stood on the rock again

strenuous teaching programme.

Then, out of the blue, Daphne telephoned me to say that a man in Neo Khorio had a daughter to marry off and was in need of some ready cash. He wanted to sell a piece of land a few hundred metres behind their country house in Neo Khorio. We drove up there and I instantly recognised it as the very place where Daphne and I had picked *glysteritha* when we visited their house for the first time. I stood on the rock again, looking out over the beautiful bay of Chrysochous. It seemed like an omen, coming at this point in time. Land was cheap in this then remote area. No one wanted to live in such an out of the way place with no good main roads and few facilities. We met the owner, Lambis, and shook hands on the deal.

I was glad of the smaller teaching commitment, which left me free to spend a great deal of time over the next couple of years travelling up and down to Paphos to get all the necessary documentation completed. We now had a dream. One day we would build a house on our land at the back of beyond. We had no knowledge, however, of just how soon that dream was to be realised.

17. LARA

One of Harry's successful ventures at the Education Centre was a series of lectures given by overseas speakers. They proved to be extremely popular and well-attended. Not surprising, really, as there were some big presenters to draw the crowds.

One such visitor was the eminent astronomer Patrick Moore. His lecture was engrossing, and the subsequent presentation he gave for schoolchildren was highly entertaining as well as informative. He had a great sense of humour and a very understanding nature. When he had a few hours free, I took him on a whirlwind shopping expedition to Limassol, and we enjoyed ourselves immensely. One evening he captained a visitors' cricket eleven against an Akrotiri side and acquitted himself well, being an extremely useful bat. At some point during the week, Harry and I accompanied him on an official visit to the resident battalion's band at Episkopi. As soon as he walked in they struck up with Star Wars at full blast. He was delighted. For the next piece, the bandmaster invited him to accompany them on the xylophone. This he did with the utmost brilliance. A most likeable man, and a gentleman of extraordinary talents.

There were also talks and slide-presentations of local interest. They included subjects like archaeology, ornithology and an all-time favourite - the turtle conservation project at Lara. Andreas Demetropoulos, the head of the Cyprus Fisheries Department, who is a superb wildlife photographer, gave a presentation with some wonderful slides. He also brought with him several turtle hatchlings from eggs which had been hatched in an incubator. He intended to release them at Lara later that evening. I was completely fascinated by these tiny, primaeval creatures. They seemed so unusual and mysterious. I longed to learn more about them.

After the lecture, when we were entertaining the speaker for supper, I actually got the chance. He invited us to go to Lara one weekend. When we had the free time we could liaise with the Paphos Fisheries Department which was responsible for the smooth running of the operation.

The following weekend we packed up the car with sleeping-bags, torches, dark clothing suitable for tracking turtles at night, and a box of provisions for the communal kitchen at Lara. With eager anticipation, we set off for Paphos - due to meet up with the Fisheries' team at the harbour. We reached the old town of Paphos, only to have the car develop a problem and come to a standstill. We knew they would be waiting for us at Kato Paphos, so while Harry tried to locate the fault, I jumped into a taxi and went down to tell them what had happened.

Nothing ruffles the composure of Andreas the turtle

This was my first meeting with Andreas Pistentis, who remains today one of our closest friends. He was lashing cages, for covering turtle nests, on to a trailer behind a big Toyota Landcruiser when I showed up with my sob-story. Nothing ruffles the composure of Andreas the Turtle. He unhitched the trailer, drove me back to the town, then disappeared momentarily and came back with a mechanic who would repair the car and keep it for the weekend. Loading us and all our gear into his vehicle, he returned to the harbour for the trailer. The second vehicle, with the rest of the equipment, had already left for Lara. One last check and then we were on our way to the Turtle Hatchery.

It was the first time I had been out on to the Akamas. The track following the coast was narrow and deeply rutted. The British army kept it in a reasonable state of repair as they were virtually the only other people to use it. The big Landcruiser rode the bumps with ease, and from our high position in the vehicle, we had a clear view of the wild and beautiful peninsula around us. On our left the sea sparkled deeply blue beyond a line of white surf which rolled in over a long sandy beach at a place called Toxeftra. Andreas pointed out several tracks which looked as if they had been made by the heavy tread of a tractor - the unmistakable signature the breeding turtle leaves when she comes ashore to lay. On our right the wind had carved intricate and picturesque shapes in the sandstone cliff. The ground was covered in dense scrub. Trees, where they managed to grow, were leaning at an angle - bent over before the fury of winter winds blasting in from the sea. Lizards, basking in the sun on the dirt road, scuttled away as we approached, and once or twice, snakes slithered out of sight into the bushes as we passed.

We turned off the main track into the dunes, following a route marked only by the tyres of the Fisheries vehicles. After several twists and turns we came to a halt at the top of a fairly steep cliff and, climbing out of the car, looked down upon an incredibly beautiful bay with a beach of fine golden sand. This was Lara, the main breeding ground of the endangered sea-turtle. Below us, at the back of the beach, was a small encampment. A wooden hut with a verandah constituted the kitchen and dining area, and there was an outside sink for washing-up. A few yards away a shower had been rigged up. Every drop of fresh water had to be brought in containers to refill a large storage tank. In fact everything that was used at Lara had to be manhandled up and down the steep cliff path - a tiring job in the extremely hot conditions. Two large tents, in which several safari beds had been set up, provided sleeping accommodation, and in front of them there was a spacious rattan shelter. I immediately knew I was going to love staying here.

Giorgos, one of the team from the Fisheries Department at Nicosia, was resident at the hatchery for the whole of the season. He came forward to greet us as we reached the camp. A rather quiet man, he was an expert in turtle-tracking and a great cook.

In front and to the left of the camp was a roped-off area. Here nests were dug in the warm sand to incubate eggs which had been collected from other beaches. They perfectly imitated those dug by the turtles themselves and they were all covered with circular wire cages and labelled. The wild nests of turtles, which came ashore to lay on this particular beach, were similarly covered and marked in situ.

Over the next couple of days I was to learn the system that was used to record all the relevant information on the turtles that came ashore. For now, there was a lot of unloading of equipment and stores to help with before we dived into the shallow breakers to cool off.

As evening approached, we chose our beds and changed into turtle-tracking gear. Then it was all hands to help Giorgos with the preparations for dinner. There was plenty to discuss as we sat on the verandah looking out over the sea. A hush fell as the sun began to go down behind the horizon. The sunsets at Lara are magical. Sky and sea turn to crimson, red and shimmering gold and there is silence save for the sound of the surf. There is an air of expectancy, for you know that turtles are swimming restlessly around in the bay waiting for night to fall before coming secretively ashore.

Andreas lit the big hurricane lamp over the verandah and turned it down low. Soon it was time to eat. Whatever simple meal was prepared at Lara, it always tasted better than any gourmet cooking. The very simplicity of this outdoor way of life appealed to me immensely. Willing hands helped with the washing-up, and then the equipment needed for the night's work was checked. There were pencil torches, taped over so that only a pinhole of light could show, and a special instrument for fixing tags to the turtles. Walkie-talkie radios were tested and then there was nothing for it but to settle back to talk quietly or play cards until it was time for the first patrol.

Some time before eleven o'clock we set off in single file along the firm sand close to the waterline. The moon had not yet risen, but there was enough starlight to enable us to see the tracks made by the turtles. No fresh tracks showed on the damp sand and we turned at the end of the beach and retraced our steps. Several more patrols along this stretch of sand would be made tonight, but now we would clamber through the rocks on to the completely deserted beach adjoining the camp site.

The salt-scented night air was warm on our faces as we climbed over rocks and stepped around small pools. We trudged steadily along the long curve of the beach - the only sound the light scrunch of our feet on the sand and the hiss of the waves as they ran ashore. At the far end of the bay we sat down to wait before making the return journey. I lay back on the sand, looking up at the clear night sky. Bejewelled with stars, it was breathtakingly beautiful. A streak of brilliant light suddenly shot across the sky. It was gone in a second and I wondered if I were seeing things. Then Harry exclaimed as another shooting star streaked overhead.

As we sat there, the moon rose above the cliff behind us, bathing the lonely beach with silvery light. Within minutes, Andreas sat up, touched my shoulder and pointed. About twenty metres away from us a large sea-turtle had materialised in the white line of surf. She remained motionless for a few seconds at the water's edge, her gleaming wet carapace reflecting the moonlight. I was overcome with awe at the sudden appearance of the beautiful primordial creature - aware that this ancient reptilian order had been on earth long before homo sapiens had evolved. Now the increasing encroachment of man, seeking sandy beaches for the development of tourism, threatened her very existence.

She began to drag herself laboriously up the beach, leaving the tell-tale tracks deeply imprinted in the sand behind her. When she was about eighty metres or so from the sea, she began to dig. We could hear sand and small pebbles being thrown by her powerful front flippers. Now and then she paused to suck in air with a tortuous, rasping breath. We stayed where we were. Chelonia mydas, the green turtle, seeks a deserted place to breed and is easily disturbed by people, lights and noise. We knew that once the laying process had begun the turtle would be compelled to finish.

When he estimated that enough time had passed, Giorgos, silently crawled nearer to check whether she had started to lay. Soon a thin beam of light from his torch signalled that it was safe for us to approach with caution. We followed Andreas - face down in a prone position - inching our way forwards on our elbows.

I will never forget the emotion that flooded over me at the sight of the turtle in the deep hollow it had made. She was clearly visible in the bright moonlight as she deposited her eggs, one by one, into the nest-hole. She raised her head and I saw that large tears trickled from her eyes. It was as if she wept with an inconsolable sadness. We continued to watch while she completed her task. She rested only briefly, then, with her short rear flippers, began to fill in the cylindrical cavity which held the eggs. She patted the damp sand down firmly before moving forwards and beginning to throw dry sand behind her with long sweeps of her large front flippers. Finally she was satisfied and, without once looking back, she began her long haul down to the sea.

Andreas quickly marked the nest with a short piece of bamboo, for in the morning it would make the location of the hundred or so eggs easy for whoever was detailed to bring them to the hatchery. Then it was time to take her measurements and tag her. From end to end, she was just over a metre in length. I helped to stay her while Giorgos deftly fixed the tag. She offered little resistance to our ministrations and did not appear to flinch when the plastic strip was attached to her flipper. We stepped back and she began to head for the sea again. Less weighty, now that she was unencumbered with eggs, and with the route slightly downhill, she was able to move more easily. She reached the waterline and a long wave streamed over her, washing away the sand and tears. Her lovely white markings showed clearly against the shining dark-green shell. She moved swiftly forward through the foaming surf. The water swirled over her and she was gone.

I was deeply moved by the encounter, and very much aware that sea turtles, in this one's image, had been coming ashore to nest on this beach for many thousands of years. Andreas told me that the tears shed by the turtle were simply a natural defence mechanism to prevent the eyes from drying out during its enforced stay on dry land. But for me, seeming to be symbolic of their plight, the tears of the breeding turtle are one of the most poignant sights I have ever witnessed.

18. A TRIO OF TORTOISES

We were to return to the turtle hatchery many times over the next three years. It was a part of the wild peninsula where we would one day build our home. We never tired of exploring the area with Andreas as our guide, penetrating the wilderness and familiarising ourselves with various landmarks. Sometimes, as dusk fell, we would take the rough back route from Lara across to Neo Khorio and down to the beach at Asprokremma. Carefully wedged in the back of the Landcruiser would be containers of turtle hatchlings to be released there after dark. We grew to love the mountains and the forest, and never ceased to be amazed at the matchless beauty of the views in all directions. The Akamas has a grandeur and magnificence that is unique.

Back at Akrotiri we lived a completely different life. It was busy and enjoyable and we felt that, in the circumstances, we had the best of both worlds.

One day the Padre dropped by for a cup of coffee. He knew I was interested in turtles and casually mentioned that he had a couple of tortoises in need of a good home. We had loads of garden space in which they could be secured and the climate was ideal. To be truthful, I was rather pleased to take them on. The Padre brought the tortoises to us that very evening. They were enormous - at least twice the size of the ones I had been used to in the UK. I examined them both thoroughly. At his quizzical look I explained that when I was young, my father had taken me to buy a pet tortoise. At the shop there had been about a hundred of the things, all more or less identical, trundling about in a large pen. I spent ages in an agony of indecision. Was this one prettier than that one? Did I really prefer these markings to those? In the end my father began to grow impatient, so I hastily picked one up - instantly confident no other would do. When we arrived home I put my new pet down on the lawn for my mother to admire. It began to amble towards the flower-bed, but kept tilting sharply to one side as it went. From all the dozens of tortoises in that pet shop, I had chosen one that had only three legs. I seem to have some kind of genius for this sort of thing - hence my careful leg count of these two monsters. I did not want a repeat performance of poor old Peg-Leg's lop-sided existence.

Harry quickly made them a wooden housing, to provide shade and a place to sleep, and we begged some clean straw from the stables to strew inside. We buried a large shallow dish for drinking and bathing and put some low plastic fencing around to keep them from wandering out of the garden. Once I had found some fresh lettuce and other salad vegetables for their supper, they were ready to take up residence.

They seemed unperturbed by their journey in a

large cardboard box. As soon as they were released into their new quarters they began chomping on the lettuce leaves and appeared perfectly at home. As the sun began to go down, they made their way into the little wooden hut.

It was Saturday, and that night there was a party in the Mess. It went on into the early hours and we didn't get to bed until after three. We were woken somewhere around five o'clock in the morning by a persistent banging and knocking. Harry, bleary-eyed, sat up and held his head.

"What silly, inconsiderate nincompoop is nailing up boxes at this hour on a Sunday morning?"

(Well OK, he may have used a more graphic expression but this is a family book).

The noise continued. We weren't the only ones being disturbed. Various genteel admonitions to the culprit were coming from neighbouring houses.

"Belt up."

"Knock it off."

"What the hell's going on?"

The knocker-up was obviously a pretty thick-skinned individual. The banging increased in pace. Then, just as Harry was reaching for a pair of shorts, it stopped abruptly. Silence reigned and we slept until after seven o'clock.

It was hot outside as we sat on the verandah sipping our morning tea. I glanced into the tortoises' enclosure. They were both standing in the shallow dish of water and appeared contented with their lot.

Harry was making some toast and I joined him in the kitchen to set a tray for breakfast. There was no breath of wind, so we decided to sit inside the house beneath the large ceiling-fan to eat. I had just spread some of Skevoulla's home-made apricot jam on my toast when the knocking and banging started up again. It sounded very near indeed - in fact it appeared to be coming from a few feet away.

We stood up and went outside. Inside the fenced area, the slightly smaller of the two tortoises was violently ramming the shell of the larger one. The victim went off at a run but its tormentor pursued it relentlessly, aiming vicious blows and taking care to retract its head inside its shell just before the impact.

We looked at each other in bewilderment. The blighters didn't even like each other. Were we going to have them continuously at war? I wondered what our neighbours were going to say when they realised who was to blame for the racket in the night.

There was a pause in the banging as the larger tortoise became trapped against the fencing. With remarkable speed considering its reputation for tardiness, the other one nipped behind and mounted it. They were mating! At least the male was. The female didn't want to know. We didn't know whether to leave them together or keep them in separate enclosures. Then we thought it might be pretty novel to have tortoise eggs hatching out in the garden and a load of baby tortoises running around. We made the decision to leave them as they were.

The banging went on almost non-stop all day. Various neighbours showed up during the course of the morning to find out what was going on. The smaller children were fascinated.

"What are they doing, Mrs Hawkins?"

"I don't know. Let's ask your Mum, she knows all about tortoises."

The buck neatly passed, I put up with the glares of one or two friends who now found themselves with a tricky bit of explaining to do on the sex life of the tortoise. No wonder the vicar had got rid of them. By the evening I was feeling really sorry for the female. I wondered why she didn't just turn round and bash the unwelcome suitor with her shell to see how *he* liked it. She was bigger than him, after all. As it happened, she had an even better plan.

At dusk there were quite a few people sitting on our verandah drinking sundowners and watching the pantomime. At last the big tortoise headed for the wooden house - the smaller one hot on her heels. There was something of a commotion inside. It seemed he wasn't prepared to let her alone even when it was time to go to sleep. Suddenly the female appeared in the doorway again and mounted upon her back was the triumphant male. His neck was stretched up and he was uttering a weird, prolonged cry.

His ecstasy was rather short-lived, however. She came out at a run and, in his elevated position, there was no room for him to come through the low doorway as well. His head crashed into the lintel above the door and he was wiped off on to his back, where he lay, piteously waving his legs in the air, unable to right himself.

Six grown men winced, while six jubilant ladies smiled.

"Serve the blighter right..."

Early the next morning we were again woken by the banging, but this time there appeared to be a loud echo after each knock. When we looked over the verandah we could scarcely believe our eyes. The female was being subjected to the usual violent attentions of the male, and behind him, there was an even smaller tortoise bashing *his* shell. Heaven knows where he had suddenly come from. He was considerably smaller than the others, but what he lacked in size he made up for in energy.

We now had double the noise pollution problem, for this one followed the other two around everywhere. Whatever the male tortoise had must have been catching. The three of them shunted along like a little train with the carriages reducing in size towards the back. Every time the male banged against the female's shell, the newcomer instantly gave him a good whack in the same place.

Like a little train

This was getting ridiculous. Immediate action was called for. Our place suddenly seemed to have become a dumping ground for mad tortoises. I decided to do a bit of dumping myself. I approached a friend who had three small children and asked her whether she would like a pair of tortoises complete with house to live in. She was delighted. Mind you, she lived far enough away not to have heard the shell-hammering. I wasn't completely heartless - I kept the smallest one. I reckoned he would be fine without the bad example set by the big male. I was not to know that this one had even worse psychological problems of his own. He needed a name, so as practically everyone we knew seemed to be called Andreas, we called him Andreas too.

Andreas the tortoise was very tame. He never attempted to run away, in fact he insisted in coming in to the house at night to sleep. This proved to be a bit of a nuisance when we had a party going. He was always wandering about between people's feet and tripping them up, so we Sellotaped a large red rosette (like those used in gift-wrapping) on to his back to make him more visible. Our friends soon got used to him and he never seemed to get trodden on.

He did have one big problem, though. He was madly in love with the cat. Let's face it, the romance was never going to get off the ground, but the cat couldn't stand him in any case.

At night, when it was time to settle down,

Andreas always made a bee-line for a big, fluffy sheep-skin rug in front of the fireplace. Unfortunately this had already been bagged by the cat, who didn't think much of the tortoise muscling in. She showed her disapproval by swiping him with her front paw and turning her back on him. This only served to increase his ardour, and much to her annoyance, he followed her everywhere she went. Maybe she reminded him of his mother, for all he wanted to do was to cuddle in to her to go to sleep. Perhaps it had something to do with the cat's colouring. She was mainly white with significant tortoiseshell markings. Whatever it was, he never gave up hope. The only way she could escape from his attentions was to jump up on to a chair, or if they were in the garden, sit on a tree-stump where he couldn't reach her. Even then he tried his best, standing on the very tips of his toes and straining upwards. She'd box his ears for him again, but he never gave up.

When winter came and there was a log fire burning in the big stone fireplace, the cat was reluctant to move from her cosy rug at night. Andreas had no intention of hibernating like a normal tortoise, and eventually she was forced to allow him to share her bed. Never satisfied with just lying next to her, he would gradually insinuate himself inside the natural curve her body made when she curled herself up. Then he'd with-draw his head inside his shell and go to sleep.

Andreas remained a quirky, but much-loved, member of the family until the end of our tour. Then, like the cat, he was handed on to other pet-lovers who had just been posted in. Meanwhile, it was quite pitiful to hear the latest poor devils, who had been lumbered with the Padre's pets, pleading with newcomers and passers-by.

"Anyone like a pair of breeding tortoises?"

* * * * *

Soon after we rid ourselves of the shell-bangers we got roped in to becoming film extras in a BBC television series called 'Squadron'. It was a bundle of fun to do, and in addition we were paid for our time. Filming was mainly on location at Akrotiri, and people from the village, with their Mediterranean complexions, were ideally suited to playing the parts of South American peasants. Harry and Jeremy were cast as part of a foreign archaeological team which was caught up in someone else's war. They deserved an Oscar for their dramatic acting when they got shot. Marlon Brando would have been proud of them. They wore their realistic blood-stained bandages with real style, and the brave way in which they dragged themselves to the helicopters sent in to rescue them brought tears to your eyes.

My bit of action was on the airfield, and then it was their turn to laugh. I was cast as one of a number of peasants who arrived in busloads, all trying to get on the last plane out of the country. Two or three traditional village buses had been hired for the occasion and trans-

He was madly in love with the cat

formed with fake South American town names and number plates. Dressed in colourful peasant clothing and carrying a large cloth bundle, I climbed aboard one of them. Our instructions were to disembark in a panic as soon as the bus stopped and rush towards a big Hercules aircraft which was standing on the runway. The special effects team had been busy booby-trapping the dispersal pan beforehand, and as we ran wildly towards the aircraft, loud explosions all around us simulated an air attack. Bits of cork and clouds of dust and debris were flying in all directions.

One small lady from the village, who got out of the bus right in front of me, took her acting seriously. She leapt down and ran so fast that she tripped and did a spectacular swallow-dive before falling flat on her face. She was on the ground, her forehead bleeding and all the breath knocked out of her body, when the director boomed through his megaphone in an ultra-English upper-class accent.

"I say, that was *very* good. Could you do it again?"

Once the poor lady had been carted off for some first-aid, we did a few more takes and then the posh voice was aimed in my direction. It even knew my name.

"Can you go to wardrobe, please, Sheila. I'm going to turn you into the rich man's girlfriend."

Now my task was to dash across the airfield and sit in the front seat of a small aircraft which was waiting, its engine running, on the edge of the runway. I was to leave my leg hanging down outside the door, and as soon as I climbed in the tiny plane would take off.

In actual fact, and much to their chagrin, they were refused permission to actually take off because it would breach all kinds of safety regulations. They had to make do with one of their designers (who, as luck would have it, had a private pilot's licence) revving it up and taxiing off into the sunset with the door still open.

"That's it," bellowed the director. "That leg is nice and long, make sure you keep it in view as we go out of shot."

OK, so the legs weren't exactly supermodel class, but I was rather attached to them. I didn't much fancy the idea of having one severed by an aeroplane door. I glanced left at my South American boyfriend, the designer pilot.

"Er, how do I keep the door open against the wind as you pick up speed?"

"Just push against it with your hands."

I pushed. It felt like a ton weight and we weren't even moving. This was my moment of stardom, though. All the BBC viewers in Britain were going to be looking at *my* leg. This was no time to be a wimp.

The black and white striped clapper-board marking the takes clacked, and all hell broke loose again. Bombs and shells exploded on the airfield and make-believe peasants ran amok. The little plane's engine roared and I held the door in a vice-like grip. The designer addressed me as he opened the throttle.

"Whatever you do, don't laugh. Act terrified."

Act terrified? Hellfire, I *was* terrified. He hurtled across the runway while I valiantly hung on to the door, to stop it from closing on my well-photographed leg. I trusted the Wing Commander, who had refused permission for this guy to take off, would soon be promoted to Group Captain.

The film was duly shown in the UK, and shortly afterwards we obtained a copy on video tape. A crowd of us gathered around the Mess television. Loud cheers greeted the pseudo archaeologists' performances. My moment of glory was the very last shot in the film. Suddenly, there was the little aircraft standing on the runway. It looked miles away. You could just about make out that the door was partly open. Then, before you could blink, it shot forward and out of sight. That was it. My leg never became famous and I never got any film offers. The archaeological stars went around with smug expressions of satisfaction on their faces.

I still had the last laugh, though. By the time they got round to shooting my bit, the Cypriot extras were getting dissatisfied with the amount of time they had to spend on location each day. They wanted more money. The director couldn't afford to do a complete reshoot, so he gave in to their demands.

When I went to collect my dues at the end of the day, the girl handing out the cash said that as everyone else on the last take was getting the new rate, I was entitled to it as well. She smiled and handed me an envelope containing exactly double the amount the others had earned.

19. FLAMENCO HARRY

Sometimes when we stayed at Lara, the sponge-divers' big wooden boat would call in and anchor in the bay for the night. We came to know them well, and it was always interesting to go aboard and inspect their haul. Unfortunately, mishaps were wont to occur with the sometimes antiquated equipment used by the divers.

Our good friend and next door neighbour at Akrotiri, Ken, was the administrator for the RAF hospital. One day, when he came home for lunch, he told us that one of the divers had been brought in by helicopter from Latchi that morning. He had surfaced too quickly and was suffering from the bends. The RAF, immediately answering the urgent request for assistance, had airlifted the stricken man to Akrotiri, where he had been placed in the decompression chamber. Ken, also a frequent visitor to the turtle hatchery, had recognised him at once as Giorgos, one of our mutual acquaintances in the sponge-diving world. Happily his condition was not too serious and, after a night in the chamber, he was fit to be released.

Soon after Ken arrived at work the following morning, he telephoned to say that Giorgos had been cleared to go, but that he had no clothes or shoes and no means of getting back to his boat. He brought the somewhat embarrassed diver back to the house and, between them, he and Harry found him something to wear. I knew what was coming next. They were both tied up at work, so I was detailed to return him to Latchi. I didn't mind. It was a beautiful day and a trip to the Akamas beats routine household chores hands down.

Giorgos realised it had been quite a close call, and he was extremely grateful for the prompt way in which he had been rescued and expertly treated by the Royal Air Force. He appeared none the worse for his dice with death, and was keen to get back and join the other divers.

We arrived at Latchi and I drove up to the harbour and parked. I could see a dozen or more fishermen sitting at tables looking thoroughly glum and depressed. As Giorgos stepped out of the car there was a stunned silence followed by joyful shouts. Then, all at once, they surrounded him, slapping him on the back and embracing him. They had heard no news of him since he had been taken away in the helicopter. They did not know how seriously he had been affected. Indeed, they had no idea whether he was alive or dead. It was a fantastic moment.

One man was in tears. He was not a regular member of the crew, but had been helping out on the boat when the accident had occurred. He blamed himself, for on receiving a signal from the sea-bed that a basket of sponges was ready to be hauled up, he had winched up the hapless diver instead. Now tears of relief ran down his face as he saw that Giorgos was unharmed. He squeezed my hand so tightly I thought the bones would be crushed. Then all the fishermen came to shake my hand and it was time for the celebrations to begin.

Bottles of beer and *ouzo* appeared on the table. Greek music was played on a radio and two of the men began to dance while the others clapped in time to the music. One fisherman took a huge *orfos* from his morning's catch and gave it to Yiangos, the harbourmaster and restaurateur, to grill over the charcoal. They had an instant party going in about two minutes flat.

It was a memorable occasion. When I left, they crowded round the car with gifts for us and the people who had helped them. The boot was full of lovely natural sponges for the aircrew and the doctors. There were a couple of beautiful triton shells and several plastic bags of fish packed in ice.

The next time I was to meet up with these fun-loving and hospitable men was a month or so later when one of their number got married. A big wedding party was thrown at Latchi, and when we arrived, we were treated as honoured guests. Nothing was too much trouble. The usual bottles of beer were brought round and our table soon saw them off. When Harry was offered a brandy he said he'd prefer a beer. Whereupon our hosts delved under the table, saying they had their own source of supply in case of shortages. The space beneath the table was stacked with crates of Keo beer.

It was on this occasion that I had the wind taken

out of my sails somewhat. When the formalities were over and the dancing had begun in earnest, I noticed a tall and extremely good-looking fisherman glancing repeatedly at our table and smiling. Eventually he got to his feet and approached us. Being the only woman there, I assumed he was going to ask me to dance. Still smiling, he walked past me and asked Harry.

I wouldn't have minded, but he said *yes.*

* * * * *

Our own wedding anniversary came round. This time it was silver for twenty-five years. Harry, wishing to mark the occasion, said he was going to lash out on a substantial present for me. He was undecided between a canteen of silver cutlery or a Mini-moke. There was no contest as far as I was concerned. I could always eat with my fingers. I opted for the moke.

We had so much fun with that sturdy little car and it was to prove an invaluable workhorse in the years ahead. Jeremy, still under the age for driving, took great delight in being able to whiz around in it on the dropping-zone adjoining the salt lake.

I come from a large police family, and when I was seventeen, my father sent me to an old airfield with some of the police drivers in his division. They set up bales of straw as obstacles and taught me road sense as well as the rudiments of advanced driving. I became used to some pretty difficult manoeuvring and disparaging remarks.

"Whoops, you've just reversed through a plate-glass window."

"That's the third pedestrian you've killed this morning."

That initial groundwork was invaluable as well as a lot of fun. Now I did the same thing for my son - by setting up obstacles with used tyres on the salt-pan and recalling the way I had been taught.

The good life continued. The bases provided every facility for their personnel. There was a rowing club, water-ski club, sailing club - you name the club and they probably had one. There were societies and evening classes for this and that, and then, of course, there was the Mess. As well as dinner-dances, summer-balls, parties and official occasions, sporting tournaments were also organised. One of the most popular was a knock-out competition of tennis mixed doubles and croquet.

Knocking a wooden ball with a mallet on a green lawn was an enlightening experience. It seemed terribly couth, but the sound reminded me of the dreaded tortoises. I did not shine at this event. Being a hockey-player, I was always a bit too forceful in walloping the ball. Besides, too many people cheated with sly nudges of their feet. I preferred a real challenge, and Tom, my nimble partner, and I won the tennis tourney every year during that tour.

All too soon it seemed the pleasant days at Akrotiri were coming to an end. In a month or so we would be returning to the UK. Harry's new posting was to HQ Strike Command at High Wycombe. The thought of leaving the island did not fill us with panic, for in our hearts we knew that it would not be too long before we returned. We had our own piece of land and we had cemented firm friendships with many of the local people. Above all, we were drawn to the Akamas. Harry was keen to take on the challenge of building a house and knew that, living there, he would be able to give full rein to his artistic talents. As for me, the Akamas represented all that was wild and beautiful, untamed and mysterious. I couldn't wait to live there.

Soon the farewell parties and *gazomes* were all over and we were on embarkation leave. We hired a truck and loaded it with things we would not require in England, but would need when we came back. We weren't exactly sure when that would be, as Harry had not at that point applied for premature voluntary retirement, but we had faith that it would not be long.

Harry drove the truck to Neo Khorio and I followed in the Mini-moke. Andreas and Daphne had given us the use of the large cellar beneath their country house in which to store things until our return. Once we had unloaded, we went for one last look at the cherished piece of land and then on up through the village and out over the Akamas to Lara. In the small open moke, I drove ahead of Harry so as not to eat his dust. Nevertheless I was still covered with the powdery, gritty substance when we reached the turtle hatchery. It was

In the small open moke

almost noon on an August day, and the heat was intense. I thought I would never be cool again. I had left Akrotiri dressed in a clean white T-shirt, white pedal-pushers and a white cotton sun-hat. The team at Lara later told me they watched in amazement as this begrimed figure came down over the cliff, walked straight past them barely raising a hand in acknowledgement, and carried on walking, fully clothed, into the sea. I can hardly remember it, but Harry said I kept going until my hat floated off.

We stayed the night at Lara, then, in the morning, returned to Akrotiri to hand over the married quarter. Our car had been shipped home, but we still had the Mini-moke to use for our final week on the island. This was to be spent in Limassol at the family-run Astir Hotel. John, nephew of the owner, was a great friend of ours - in fact Harry had been a *koumpare* at his wedding. He was determined we should make the most of our final leave, and as a start he accommodated us in the bridal suite.

We had a great holiday. There was a roof-garden with a small swimming-pool at the hotel and we started each day off with an early morning swim. One or two well-off Arab families were in residence and they usually arrived at the pool just as we were about to take our leave. The women in the party, obviously hot in their layers of clothing, started by standing on the steps in the shallow end and cooling their feet. By day three they had ventured in up to their waists - the yards of material that constituted their dresses and veils floating around them. When the women and children got out it was the turn of the rather corpulent men. They wore what we termed *jelly-babies* - in fact they were the loose cotton robes normally worn by Arab males - *jellabas.* Underneath they were wearing full-length cotton drawers to match. Their drawers straining over their ample midriffs, they flung themselves in shrieking loudly. None of them could swim, but they all had a marvellous time laughing at each others' antics. Their laughter became almost hysterical when they got out. So did ours, for their thin drawers had become completely transparent. It was not a pretty sight, but it was extremely funny.

The day before we left, John said he was taking us out for a grand farewell. He wanted to give us a night to remember. We would dine at a well-known restaurant and then go on to Maxim's to see the cabaret. Sounded good to me, but then I didn't know that this Maxim's was not a lot like the French original.

We dined by flickering candlelight at a table overlooking the sea. The calm water was washed in moonlight and a gentle breeze carried the fragrance of night-scented flowers. It was our last night on the island and I wished it would never end.

Then we moved on to Maxim's. I should have been suspicious when the car turned into Limassol's notorious red light district. The night club was in one corner of the square and could best be described as somewhat seedy. Inside there was a small raised stage, a few tables with chairs, and at the back, a bar where three well-dressed Arabs were sitting looking bored. They ignored the attentions of several girls who were trying to persuade them to fork out the price of an air ticket to Egypt to buy them a glass of sugar-water each.

We were ushered to a table at the front by the manager, with whom John was obviously acquainted. John has a great sense of humour, and I had a feeling he intended to give us a night we would not forget in a hurry. He did. Without warning, there was a loud burst of flamenco music and a girl in a red flounced dress whirled on to the tiny stage. She was supple and not a bad dancer. I glanced at the Arab trio. They were lounging on their bar-stools watching her impassively. The in-house girls had given up on them in disgust and were sitting sulkily at one of the tables. We were the only other customers in the place.

The tempo of the music slowed and the girl began to click a pair of castanets as she circled the stage. Suddenly a figure, brightly-clad in turquoise satin, leapt through a gap in the curtains. It was a rather small, muscular man, dressed in a matador's tightly-fitting suit of lights. On his head was a black three-cornered hat. He began to beat out a tattoo with his feet and, as the tempo of the music increased, he performed a full-blooded flamenco dance. He was agile and athletic and a quite remarkable dancer.

I looked back at the Arabs again. All three were sitting upright staring intently at the act. The bored bar-girls buffed their nails and pouted. I looked at John. He grinned and said nothing. The dancer grabbed the girl in the red dress and began to twirl her around the stage, bending her supple body into all kinds of contorted positions. We applauded. Harry applauded so enthusiastically that the male dancer held out a hand and invited him up on to the stage. Harry, well-wined and dined, went. The man removed his tricorn hat and offered it to him - at the same time standing back and indicating his partner. I looked at John. His grin almost split his face in two. Now I knew why we were here.

Harry jammed the hat on his head, and looking like a slightly mad Napoleon, raised his hands above his head and stamped his size elevens in time to the music. The male dancer clapped approvingly. After a few minutes he moved forward to regain his hat. But he reckoned without Harry who by now had the bit between his teeth and wasn't going to relinquish his moment of fame so easily.

He grabbed the girl in the red dress and began to hurl her around the stage. To her credit, after the initial shock, she kept her professional smile and went along with it. Not so the lead dancer. His smile rapidly disappeared as he repeatedly tried to regain possession of his hat and his partner.

John and I were literally helpless with laughter, and even the bar-girls at their empty table were giggling. The three Arabs sat there open-mouthed. In the end, the matador had to snatch his hat from the pretender's head and whisk his partner away when Harry let go of her hand in an unguarded moment.

We sat there trying to recover our composure. Harry, as though he needed it, had another brandy to help in the process. The bar-girls surrounded the Arabs again, but they were extremely unco-operative. In fact, they were downright rude to them.

The curtains at the back of the stage parted once more and the male dancer appeared. He had changed from his matador's outfit into a body-hugging pair of white trousers and T-shirt, which showed his lithe frame off to great advantage. He stalked past our table without a glance at his stand-in and went right up to the Arabs, who embraced him fondly. Without a word being exchanged, they threw some bank notes on the counter, and with their faces wreathed in smiles, led him out of the building.

John was right about one thing. It *was* a night to remember.

20. A LAND BEYOND COMPARE

The following day we left the island. This time it was not so bad. We knew we would return - we just couldn't be sure exactly when. We left the Mini-moke in a spare garage belonging to Andreas and Daphne. How long would it be before we drove it again?

Once in England, we went straight to a married quarter at Strike Command Headquarters. The country-side was beautiful. Beech woods surrounded the area and the approach of autumn showed them at their best. It was not Cyprus, but there were lovely walks along secluded paths through the woods. I looked forward to exploring them.

Then came the first jolt. Women were advised not to walk in the woods alone. There was a mad rapist at large. There was another preying on women on the train to London. Every time we switched on the television news we were regaled with horror stories, which had become so commonplace that no one seemed to be shocked by them. Old ladies in their eighties were raped in their own homes. Children were murdered, it seemed, by the dozen. Armed robbery was an everyday occurrence, and houses needed to be made like Fort Knox to try to stop burglars from cleaning the occupants out. It was all gloom and doom: there never seemed to be any good news worth reporting. After living in Cyprus where no one needed to lock their cars, or their front doors, and banks and post offices had no grilles or security systems, it was a pretty depressing state of affairs.

Then a spell of wet weather set in. Lowering grey skies and non-stop drizzle did nothing to lift our spirits. I looked out at rain-slicked roads and trees which incessantly dripped water. In the mornings hundreds of men, huddled in air force-blue raincoats, streamed along the main road on their way to work. At the end of the day they poured out through the gates, heads down against the wind and rain, intent only on getting home again without getting soaked.

Harry enjoyed his job as Training Design Advisor, but it did not compare with his former post at Akrotiri. After a couple of months he came home and said he had decided to PVR. With only five years to go until he was due to retire anyway, Harry was entitled to apply for premature voluntary retirement. We had taken all aspects carefully into consideration. It would mean a fairly large financial sacrifice and a loss of security. It would also mean we could return to Cyprus and begin building our home. We had no aged parents that would have made it difficult for us to leave the UK. Both the children were out in the world - Karen now married and Jeremy studying hard for his degree at Manchester. They both liked the idea of having a permanent home in

Cyprus and gave us every encouragement.

In May 1984, ten months after we had flown out of Akrotiri, we finally made the break. We took three weeks to drive leisurely back, via France, Italy and Greece to the island we now felt was home. The next few years were hectic as we struggled to build ourselves a house. We had all the time in the world now, and loved every minute of it. This despite the hilarious episodes that resulted from our being at the mercy of local builders. We were drawn closely into the community by the caring people in the village and felt a strong bond with them and the land.

We acquired a couple of donkeys and had a great deal of fun with them, although the baby, Sheila, became a bit of a handful as she grew. The little Mini-moke we had left in Limassol now came into its own. It was a tough and manoeuvrable vehicle and very easy to load. It had no problem negotiating the rough track between the house in the village, where we lived, and the site where we were building our new home. Our next door neighbour once overestimated its strength, however. I had driven up behind the house to park outside the back gate, when I spotted Sheila in the driveway with an evil glint in her eye. Miffed because I hadn't taken her with me earlier, she was determined I wasn't going to get away again. She began to charge up the concrete drive towards the gate. When she cleared it, the only place to land would be in the moke with me. Luckily the engine was still running and I was in reverse gear. I

Sheila became a bit of a handful as she grew

rammed my foot on the floorboards and shot back into an electricity pole while the donkey, in a leap Red Rum would have been proud of, sailed over the gate and landed where I had been parked seconds earlier.

I sat there cursing the hee-hawing beast while Harry and Kokos, who lived next door, came dashing out to see what had happened. There was a strong piece of rounded metal acting as a rear bumper on the moke and this had been sharply bent into a v-shape and jammed against the bodywork by the impact.

"No problem," said Kokos helpfully. "I'll pull it straight with the tractor."

He looped a piece of chain around the metal fender and attached the other end to his tractor. He revved the engine loudly and pulled me backwards down the lane.

"Keep your foot on the brake while I pull," he yelled above the roar of the motor. I gripped the steering wheel and pressed down hard on the foot-brake.

Kokos nodded approvingly and put his foot on the accelerator. The tractor leapt forward and I sat there, while he clanked down the lane dragging the chain, bent fender and a sizeable chunk of the moke's bodywork with him.

I glanced at Harry.

"I told you I made a good job of those brakes," he said.

We became used to the unpredictable, and soon learned to be extremely wary of anyone who said "no problem".

The village was full of characters, all of them interesting. Most were idiosyncratic and quintessentially Cypriot. Some were funny and one or two were rather sad. One such sad person was Elisavou. At seventy, she was still a child of nature. She wandered freely in the village and slept among the long grasses in the dried river-bed. Sometimes she made a sleeping-place in the forest with only the cackling chukar and wild black francolin for company. All doors in the village were open to her and she wandered in at will. It always startled me to turn from the kitchen sink and bump into her, as she stood solemnly regarding me without expression.

She was small and frail. A shabby black dress hung loosely around her slight frame, the hem reaching down to her bare feet. She never wore shoes, neither in summer nor in winter. Her feet were cracked, leathery and begrimed with the dirt of ages. She did not cover her head with the *mandila* worn by other village women. Instead, lank, grey hair, unwashed and unkempt, framed her thin face. Her general appearance was one of uncleanliness and neglect. Only the eyes seemed alive, glittering darkly from within sunken eye-sockets.

The first time she came I asked what I might offer her. She did not reply but her gaze wandered to a colander of freshly-washed tomatoes on the draining-board. They were ripe and succulent with droplets of water adhering to their smooth, red skins. I selected one and offered it to her. A claw-like hand, the nails rimed with dirt, reached out from the voluminous folds of her stained dress to take it. She appraised the offering, then abruptly returned it to me without comment.

I proffered some bread topped with sesame seeds. She ignored me. I was at a loss. We stood there, face to face, for what seemed like an eternity. Finally, she made for the door, her bare feet making no sound on the tiled floor. She stepped outside, then turned towards me again. She spoke with a thick regional accent, her voice quavering and reedy.

"Eshis veloni, kori?"

Did I have a needle? Why on earth should she want a needle? When I replied in the negative she turned her back and, without another word, padded silently away. I was intrigued by this lonely, lost soul. I asked about her. What was her history? Had she no family? Why did she always ask me for needles?

It seemed she was indeed alone in the world, but every time an attempt was made to bring her permanently back to the village, she resisted it. She continued to come and go as she pleased. The village women fed her, and when she fell ill, bathed her and looked after her, but as soon as she was well enough she would be off again to wander in the forest. Gifts of shoes were immediately discarded - she preferred to go barefoot.

What, then, was the significance of the needles? She told the women she must always have one in case she should tear her dress on the thorn bushes in the forest. Of course, she never did repair her ragged dress and lost the needles almost as soon as she was given them. Nevertheless, a shining new needle, laid in the palm of her small hand, gave her great comfort and she never stopped asking for them until the day she died.

Her lifeless body was found huddled, like a bundle of rags, on the floor of an old house in the village, on a cold and windy January day. The sun was shining and the sea, beneath its plunging white horses, was coloured in every shade of blue, green and turquoise imaginable. Long breakers of thundering surf crashed on the beach, sending sprays of white foam high in the air.

Poor Elisavou. In the spring I went to the tiny burial ground. A pathetically small mound of earth marked her final resting place. I made my way to the derelict house where she had been found. It lay empty and desolate in the warm sunshine. A sudden breeze gusted, rattling a wooden window-frame, and a loose shutter banged to and fro. Dust swirled and eddied on the stone-flagged floor. Perhaps it was a figment of my imagination but the wind, sighing through the narrow gaps where the walls met the sagging roof-beams, seemed to call to her. Mournful, sibilant, it whispered her name. *El-eee-ss-ssav-oouu.* No answer came from the silent house. Only a wild dove, roosting in a crevice in the ruin, heard the eerie cry and began to utter its own soft, sad lamentation.

A decade later I wrote a book about our experiences, and amazingly it became a best-seller in Cyprus. Two years later I found myself with a new career as author and journalist, when the Cyprus Mail, the longest-established English language newspaper on the island, published my second book and asked me to write a monthly column in the Sunday edition.

* * * * *

In the first two books I wrote about a rapidly-disappearing way of life. Now, with the new millennium, the rate of progress has quickened apace. Startling changes are taking place as the population becomes more affluent and the island is opened up even more for tourism. For the most part, as the older residents of the villages age and die, their picturesque stone-built houses are torn down and replaced with modern villas or apartment complexes. The sound of earth movers heralds the fall of much fertile, arable land to the developers. A mountain near Androlikou, the village of the goats, has been moved - blown apart by dynamite - the ancient limestone crushed into aggregate and sand for building. Even recently-discovered fossils in a reef, laid down by the living coral in warm, shallow water aeons ago, will disappear into the gaping maw of the great God of Construction. At a mere fifteen million years old, they are not considered important enough to be worth preserving.

Village men no longer wear the *vraka,* and many of the old customs are becoming a thing of the past. National dress is seen only in hotels, when a new generation performs traditional dances for tourists. Donkeys, one of the most endearing attractions for urban visitors to Cyprus, are fading from the scene. They have outlived their usefulness and are being replaced by modern machinery. Thankfully a few remain in more remote villages like ours - most of them more photographed than the queen.

Yet still this lovely island has a magic of its own. It is unique - a land beyond compare. Sometimes, amid the hurly-burly of city life, it may be difficult to appreciate the beauty and the wonders to be seen. But if you seek out the mountains and the forest, deep hidden valleys or the coast, then here they surely are. Here too the steadfast people I have come to love. For the heart of Cyprus lies in the people from its villages. They are the very essence of the land - the salt of the earth. Roots go deep on this island. The Cypriot has a passion for the homeland, a deep and lasting bond that is so rarely understood by strangers. Pride and love of country shine from weatherbeaten faces. They have a word that is difficult to translate. *Kopiaste.* It means come and sit with me and share what I have. As little as they may have, they will share it with the *xenos.*

One such man, whom I shall never forget, was Panayiotis from Polemi. We had heard about a man living there who was a hundred years old and still working his land. His reputation went before him, and locally he was known as the Century Man. One day, late in the morning, we stopped at the coffee shop in Polemi and

Locally he was known as the Century Man

enquired where we might find him. Several of the old men sitting there answered at once. They urged us to sit and have coffee - Panayiotis would arrive shortly to partake of his mid-day meal.

We sat, drinking our *metrios* and chatting to them. After a while one of them pointed along the road. Coming towards us, carrying a pick, a scythe and a *tappas,* was the man we had come to see. This was no wizened, white-haired old man. Upright in stance, he was lean and fit-looking, his eyes clear and alert. A full head of iron-grey hair and a beard, sprinkled with lighter grey, framed his tanned face.

He placed the tools against the wall and sat down at one of the small tables. His compatriots told him we had come from the Akamas to see him. The Englishman was an artist and would like to draw him. He greeted us politely and listened to what they had to say as the *kafejis* placed a cup of coffee in front of him. He spread a clean napkin on the table and took some bread, ripe tomatoes and a whole *halloumi* from a plastic bag. With a sharp knife he methodically cut the food into portions, before looking directly at us and saying "*kopiaste*". He was engaging and intelligent, with a mind and body any man half his age would have been proud of. It was a privilege to meet him, and although he died a year or so later, he remains one of the most unforgettable characters I have ever met.

The generous nature and hospitality of the Cypriot is unrivalled anywhere in the world. They also have an innate sense of humour which draws me to them. One Easter some friends came on holiday from the UK. Theodosis suggested we bring them to his house to see the preparations for the festivities. Several members of his family had gathered in the small kitchen and the women were making *flaounes* and boiling eggs in water containing a red vegetable dye. Chrissie, the matriarch, made the visitors so welcome they were all but overwhelmed.

We sat in the tiny courtyard as decorative Easter loaves were loaded into the big outdoor oven. The head of the English household, appreciatively sipping his coffee, remarked on Chrissie's warm and welcoming attitude. He told me to ask Theodosis whether he could take her home with him when he went. When I translated this for Theodosis, a wicked glint came into his eye. He glanced at the Englishman's attractive, and considerably younger, wife, and replied with a straight face.

"Certainly - as long as he leaves his wife here for me."

He came back with an even quicker riposte once, when the men in the village were taking a look at *The Back of Beyond* for the first time. Theodolous preened himself.

"That's me on the front cover."

"So what?" said Theodosis. "I'm inside."

He opened the book at the page where he is depicted with my namesake, the baby donkey, and held it up for all to see.

"So he is," I said, adding cheekily: "Theodosis is the one with the hat on."

As quick as a flash he retorted.

"Yes, and the donkey's name is Sheila."

Too old now to really earn a good living from his land, this old shepherd, like many others, gets by on the small pension paid by the government. They have little in the way of the material goods the rest of us take for granted. Yet, when he heard one day that we were unexpectedly faced with a very large medical bill, this kind and caring man, who treats me as one of his family, took my arm and lowered his voice.

"Sheila, I know that doctors cost a lot of money. I have two hundred pounds in the bank. It is yours if you need it."

It was literally all he had saved over the years from his back-breaking toil, yet he would willingly have given it to me. It made me weep.

Where else in the world, but in a small Cypriot community, do you go shopping to be offered coffee by those who serve you? Where everyone laughs when you are happy and comforts you when you are sad. Where actions take the place of meaningless words when practical help is needed. Where else can you find this sense of belonging? All over Cyprus, particularly in the more isolated villages, I have found this same desire and willingness of the people to be friends. They have a frank and open curiosity - unlike Europe where we do not trust strangers. Where, indeed, we may well fear them if we encounter them in a lonely place.

We made a new friend in a lonely place in the spring. We had gone to find the 16th century Byzantine monastery of Panayia tou Sinti. Uninhabited and remote, it lies at the bottom of a deep valley beside the Xeros river. From the hill village of Pentalia we followed a narrow concrete road which soon petered out into a dirt-track. The land immediately below the village was extensively cultivated. Grape vines were planted alongside almond and olive trees, and salad vegetables were plentiful. People hoeing weeds straightened up from their toil to wave to us and call a cheery greeting. Several working donkeys were tethered in the fields and goats bleated in a nearby *mantra.*

The dirt-track wound its way down around a huge river-basin. The topography was somewhat reminiscent of an extinct volcano. The slopes, covered in ripening grass which rippled in the warm breeze, seemed gently contoured rather than rugged. Here and there attractive outcrops of coloured rock glowed in the sunlight. Far below us, a ribbon of silver revealed the river snaking its way through the valley.

A woman, riding side-saddle on a donkey, came towards us driving a small flock of goats ahead of her. A clean white *mandila* covered her hair and her white teeth gleamed evenly in her nut-brown face as she greeted us. She approved of our visit to the monastery and told us to be sure to go inside and see the icon of the Panayia.

Uninhabited and remote

We rolled slowly on down the twisting road while crested larks rose up from the grass to perch on rocks and watch us pass. The monastery, which from the top had resembled an indistinct farm building, was now clearly visible. It stood alone beside the river on well-tilled land that was sparsely dotted with olive trees.

Turning a sharp corner for the final descent, we came across a lone figure carrying a heavy metal canister. His name was Loucas and he told us he worked for the mosquito control team. He sat on a hillock to rest while we carried on down the track which was now strewn with rocks and boulders. Along the route wild oleander was coming into flower in a profusion of glorious pink. The car bumped through a small gully, and then we were at the monastery itself.

The buildings had been constructed from natural stone found in the river-basin, and the church and cloisters were enclosed within four walls. The monastery had been long derelict, but a programme of renovation had begun to restore its former beauty. The morning sun highlighted the new terracotta roof tiles, and cast deep shadows under sandstone arches. A fig tree flourished near the main entrance and an orange tree still bore ripe fruit nearby. In the stone-paved courtyard a few scarlet poppies bloomed in mud-filled crevices. There was a deep well in the centre of the yard, and a traditional bread-oven formed one corner of the outer walls.

Inside the church it was cool and dark. It was

We came across a lone figure

empty of pews and the stone-flagged floor was bare. There was a faint smell of incense, and several candle-wax effigies, brought by sick pilgrims in search of a cure, hung on a piece of cord behind the heavy wooden door. Raised up on a stand in front of a flickering candle was the revered icon of the Panayia. A solid silver mount enclosed the likeness and the eternal Mother and child gazed out at the world with untroubled serenity.

I closed the door behind me, quietly enjoying the sense of isolation and tranquillity. A little way along the wide riverbank stood the ruin of an old water-mill, while on the other side, the inhospitable mountain stretched up to Vrechia, Panayia and beyond. Behind me I could see Loucas, sitting on the hillside, silhouetted against the skyline. He stood up as we approached.

"This is for you," he said.

He held out a *vrougalli* - a small hand-brush he had made from tough wiry grass while he waited patiently for a lift back up to Pentalia. It was intricately knotted and he had attached a plaited carrying-handle so that it could be hung up on a hook. He told me they were widely used in the village and were extremely useful for small sweeping jobs. With a broad grin he gave me a brief demonstration of its capabilities. I thanked him. I won't be using it, though. I shall keep it always as a reminder of his kindness and the friendship so freely given by the Cypriot people.

21. A FISHY BUSINESS

It is good to be able to call on friends when you need them, and in early June I had reason to telephone an old friend.

The small Cyprus pied wheatear, who regularly uses the nest boxes we have provided around the place, chose this year to lay her eggs in the one she favours most, which is attached to the studio wall. She successfully hatched her young and was soon hurtling around catching vast quantities of food for them. She is not tame. She rather tends to ignore us - waiting until we have passed by her nest before approaching it. However, if a predator appears in the garden she will draw it to our attention by her agitated behaviour. If we do not react, she will keep it up - sometimes flying into the studio where Harry is working or coming to the kitchen window to perch on the wire outside. When we go to investigate there will be a cat crouching in the shrubbery, or a snake passing through. She never gives us a false alarm.

Thus, when she created a commotion by her nest-box I felt compelled to go and see what was up. I moved a copper tray, which was leaning against the wall, and behind it found a tiny fledgling which had fallen out of the nest. I rescued it for her but she still continued to panic. I searched among the logs which are stored underneath. Nothing. Next to the logs is a Weber barbecue kettle with a domed lid. It has adjustable air-holes, but they looked rather small for one of the baby birds to pass through. The parent was insistent. She warned and scolded from the hedge above my head. I lifted the lid off and quickly shoved it back. There was a snake curled up inside. It was not a particularly big snake and my first thought was that it was a European cat snake, for they are nocturnal and this one was sleeping. It was grey with black markings and about two or three feet long. I could not get a really good look at it in the dim interior, though, and I was a bit concerned that it might be a young viper sleeping off a heavy meal.

I rang Snake George. I knew he would want it, whatever it was, to add to the collection in his Reptile Park near Peyia. It is a fascinating place, where the snakes of Cyprus can be viewed in their natural environment. Harry came home as I replaced the receiver. He adjusted the air-holes so that the prisoner could not escape. Before long Snake George arrived. He calmly removed the lid, put his hand in and lifted out the snake.

"A beautiful cat snake," he said. "See where she has eaten a small bird."

He indicated a large bulge halfway along the reptile's length. Poor old Piedy. No wonder she had been making such a fuss. George placed his prize in a special specimen case. He put another one on the table.

"Better if I leave this one here, then you can keep things in it until I come."

"What sort of things?"

"Anything you find. Snakes, lizards, chameleons, frogs, toads, spiders..."

"George, there is no way I am going to pick up one of those African bird-eating spiders."

"OK. We will look in the traps now and see if we have any."

Months previously, he had pinched five of my small earthenware plant pots, and placing a small piece of damp cloth in each, had put them, upside-down, beneath shrubs in various locations in the garden. The females would use them to make their nests, he had said. Maybe he was right, but nothing was going to induce me to move one of them to take a look. Harry didn't seem too keen either, and they were exactly as George had left them.

I couldn't resist looking - from a safe distance behind him - while he inspected the pots. Four yielded nothing at all, but the fifth one, near the garden shower, was full of webby nesting material. The spider had legged it. I wondered where the devil she was - not to mention all her offspring. I remembered the damp mop we had disposed so many of them with. I hoped she wasn't planning the revenge of the bird-eating spider.

Snake George, a first class herpetologist, has been a friend of ours for many years. A French TV company made a documentary film of him on location in

Cyprus and it was shown on the Discovery Wildlife channel. A couple of years ago he was awarded an Honourable Mention in the Rolex Awards for Enterprise, and in 1998 the Austrian President honoured him with the country's highest scientific award in recognition of his work with the herpetology and fauna of Cyprus. It was the first time ever that the award had gone to a non-academic.

* * * * *

Sometimes I think this place is rather like a cross between a menagerie and a madhouse. As if snakes in the barbecue weren't enough, we now have frogs in the loo. The emerald green tree frog (Hyla savignyi) thrives in our garden. These tiny creatures are active at night and during the day they cling to trees in the shade, or secrete themselves in the undergrowth well away from the burning heat of the sun.

One little male in particular tends to rest up in the bathroom of Harry's studio. He usually clings to the water-pipe in the shower-stall, or sits on top of the shower hose. We became accustomed to seeing him there and when there was no sign of him for several days in a row, we presumed he had hopped it.

That is until a lady, who was visiting, asked if she might use the toilet. She disappeared into the studio bathroom, and a minute or so later we heard a shriek. She came out with an embarrassed apology, but she was afraid she couldn't abide 'creepy-crawlies'. She said she would never be able to sit on a loo in Cyprus again.

I went in and the poor little frog, who had just had the equivalent of Niagara Falls descend upon him when she flushed the loo, was clinging with his suckered feet to the smooth porcelain inside of the lavatory. It was lucky he wasn't sluiced right down into the septic tank. Once the last trickle of water stopped flowing, he climbed up in under the rim of the bowl, where he had obviously been passing his days in cool, dark, damp seclusion. I'm not sure which of them got the biggest fright, but apart from when I clean in there, I can't keep on looking to see if he is in residence. Hence the notice on the bathroom door, which reads 'BEWARE OF THE FROG'.

As to the birds which nest in and around the garden, many sceptical friends have voiced doubts about whether they are the same ones each year. It may sound ridiculous, but certainly to me, they are easily recognizable. They have definite characteristics which set them apart, and you come to know their particular calls, where they habitually perch to sing, and, most of all, their predictable behaviour.

I was pretty surprised, however, by someone else's instant recognition of a bird recently - for this bird was a vulture! A generation ago these huge birds thrived here. Now a gathering of vultures is a rare sight indeed. One colony survives protected within the Sovereign Base at Episkopi, but elsewhere in the free

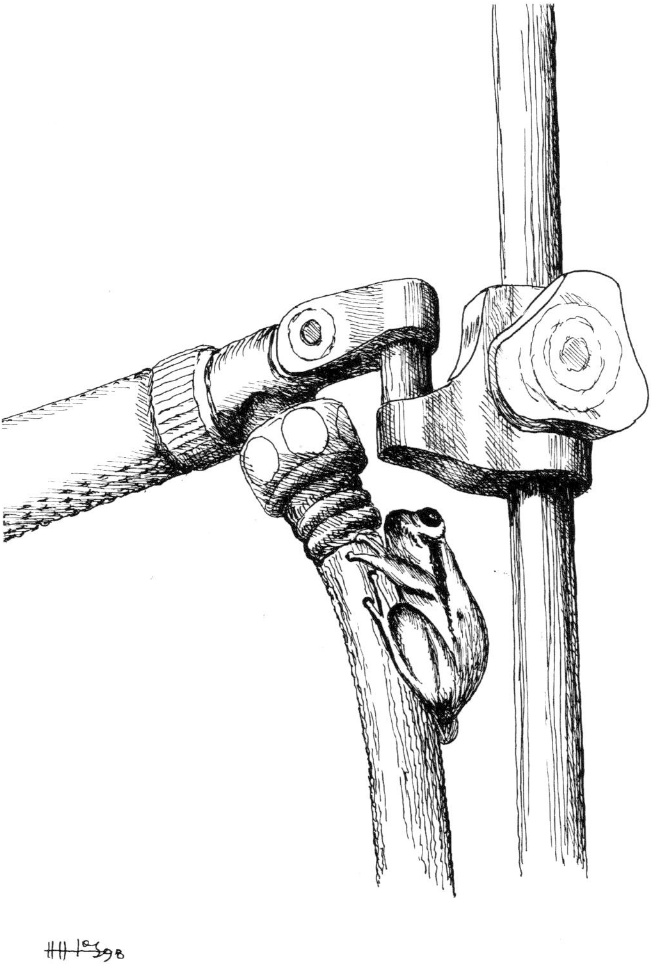

Sits on top of the shower-hose

areas of Cyprus, their very existence is threatened.

I contacted Vassos Pantelas, the senior conservator from the Forestry Department. He has a great love for his country and its flora and fauna. In an effort to increase the number of Griffons in the wild, he set up a captive breeding programme. The project is still in its infancy, but things are looking good for their future survival. He was happy for us to visit the site, and very early one morning, we made a rendezvous with the forestry officers high in the Paphos mountains. Time for a *metrio* before we transferred the photographic equipment into their vehicle. Then we set off for the isolated valley where the vultures were due to be fed at dawn. Simultaneously carcasses are laid outside the pen for the wild ones, for it is hoped that the captive birds will one day join their colony.

The white Pajero, bearing the emblem of the Forestry Department, bumped over the rough dirt road towards the bottom of the valley. Pale dust, churned up by the wheels, swirled behind us in an opaque cloud. The heat seemed oppressive after the relatively cooler air in the mountains above. We came to an abandoned Turkish village. The crumbling houses lay empty and forlorn. No hens scratched in the baked earth, and no children laughed and played in the sun. The inhabitants were long gone. The minaret of the small mosque pointed beseechingly skywards, but only the resident jackdaws, perched near the parapet, answered the silent call to prayer.

Gnarled and ancient olive trees, their boughs weighed down with plentiful green olives, waited in vain to be harvested. In the cemetery, on the outskirts of the village, rectangular tombs, constructed with multi-coloured flat stones, stood brightly out from among the dried grasses and thistles which grew around them. Large prehistoric-looking lizards sunbathed on fallen stone walls and a black snake slithered across the track, leaving its unmistakable trail in the dust.

We reached the watercourse at the bottom of the valley and then we were climbing, almost vertically it seemed, up a sharply-steeping, roughly bulldozed fire-break. At the top we left the vehicle and walked the remaining few metres to a large wire enclosure. I caught my breath at the sight of its occupants. There, with the early morning sun highlighting their plumage, were five magnificent Griffon vultures.

Andreas Stefani, our escort, unlocked the door and Harry and I stepped through to stand in the enclosure with the huge birds. Viewed from a few feet away the sheer size of them is awe-inspiring. They look pretty enormous when seen circling high above, but try a nine-foot wingspan when one is loping towards you along the ground. Now *that's* impressive, not to mention terrifying. Harry was instantly engrossed in getting some good close-up shots with his new camera. I looked intently at one vulture which was standing quietly on a log. It returned my gaze unblinkingly. I tried to memorize every detail of its symmetrical perfection. About a metre tall with a long neck and sharply-pointed, curved beak, it had its own cruel, primitive beauty. Not bald-headed, wrinkled and ugly like some vultures, this bird had a head and neck covered with white down and a creamy-white ruff encircled its throat. Its plumage was a pale golden brown, enriched with darker brown feathers flecked in places with white. Creamy-white too were the pantaloons which showed beneath. The diamond-patterned, greyish skin of its legs ended in large taloned feet which gripped the log on which it stood. The bright eyes continued to return my stare.

All at once, the bird I was so closely observing began to raise and lower its head. The movement became more violent and I wondered if this nodding was some kind of social behaviour - a greeting ritual perhaps. I soon found out how wrong I was, for suddenly it disgorged food from its over-full crop and lumps of horrendous-looking, evil-smelling meat began to fly in all directions. I mentally gave Andreas ten out of ten for staying outside the wire. He wasn't bothered by being in close proximity to the vultures - he'd obviously seen the meat-flinging procedure before. Once one started, the others all joined in. Meaty missiles whizzed slimily past me and some birds ran to pick up and swallow the unspeakable malodorous offerings regurgitated by their fellows. Later, I was to learn that this is a defence mechanism - the vulture's way of warning intruders to keep away.

When we exited the cage, Andreas drew my

«This is Vladimir»

attention and pointed. I looked up and there high above the valley, soaring in majestic solitude on a warm thermal current, was a lone Griffon vulture.

A few weeks later Vassos, who was in the Akamas to give a presentation at one of the hotels, turned up at the house. He was looking at some original drawings and came to the close-up Harry had done of one of the vultures. Clearly surprised, he glanced up and exclaimed.

"This is Vladimir. I would recognize him anywhere."

Well, Harry always gets a good likeness when he paints someone's portrait - but a vulture?

"Absolutely no doubt about it," said Vassos.

He then told us how he came to know the subject so well. Vladimir had been found, abandoned and sick, at Episkopi when he was very young. The vet from the British Base had contacted the Forestry department to see whether they could take him into their captive project and rear him. This they did and he thrived. When he was older and strong enough to survive in the wild, he was returned to the cliffs at Episkopi where, with much ceremony, he was set free and flew off into the sunset.

A happy ending, you might think. However there was one slight problem. During his spell in captivity, Vladimir had become rather tame, and every time he saw people walking along the cliff-top he zoomed in, with outstretched talons, to land beside them. This served to scare the living daylights out of people - some of whom had visions of the huge bird carrying off one of their children.

The army vet contacted the Forestry department again and explained the position. Vladimir was taken back into the captive breeding programme. He just happened to be the one standing on the log when we had been there.

"Actually," said Vassos, "there is another slight problem. A blood test has revealed that Vladimir is a female."

Vladimir, or Vladimera, is still there. It is unlikely that the wild Griffon colony in the vicinity of the project will ever accept her. She appears perfectly content, though. She will always have plenty to eat, and perhaps, one day, her offspring will soar in freedom on the warm air currents above the valley.

* * * * *

That summer Harry got hooked on fishing. Our young grandson Josh arrived, and his sole topic of conversation was river-fishing, a sport to which he had recently been introduced. Now he wanted to have a go at sea-fishing, and who better to show him the ropes than his grandfather? Well, practically anybody actually. Harry's past record at fishing doesn't even register on the Richter scale and he is renowned for having put the kiss of death on most fishing expeditions he has accompanied. For a start, in our home county of Devon, it is absolutely forbidden to say the word 'rabbit' before going fishing. This will most definitely bring bad luck down around your ears. Not only will you catch nothing, but there will also be a disaster of major proportions. Fair weather will rapidly disappear and a hurricane will centre in the English Channel. The boat will sink or you'll be attacked by a giant octopus. No Devonshire fisherman in his right mind will set out once somebody has voiced the sinister word. It is permissible to use euphemisms like bunny or cony, or even to refer to the offending creatures as 'them furry things', but never, never must you utter the dreaded word 'rabbit'.

Just why the poor little devils came to be regarded as the perpetrators of such bad luck is inexplicable to me. I've always thought they were rather sweet. Still there must be something behind it, for the first time Harry went with my brother to bring home a few salmon, he somehow managed to use the forbidden word and jinxed the whole proceedings. Everything that could go wrong did go wrong. The wind got up and the weather clamped in. Torrential rain soaked them to the skin as they tried to recover the seine net in the choppy water. It became fouled on the bottom and they were eventually forced to cut it loose, together with the anchor. It was an expensive loss and there were no salmon to bring home as compensation either. Now, if he is around when fishing trips are planned, he doesn't even bother to ask if he can go.

But this was a different kettle of fish. His grandson was looking to him and the rabbit curse probably didn't apply in Cyprus anyway. He went into the local fishing shop and bought a fishing rod small enough for the child to use. George the Fish fitted it out with hook, line and sinker and they were in business.

Fishing from the rocks became a regular pastime for the two of them, and it wasn't long before he returned to the shop and purchased a bigger rod so he could have a go as well. When Josh returned to school, he carried on fishing by himself until, one day, some local men arrived and took him under their wing. He came home muttering knowledgeably about groundbait and landing nets. The locals were experienced fishers of *kefalos,* the grey mullet, and Harry was soon equipped with a rod and reel, an old spark-plug for a weight and a bag of bread rolls for bait.

You entice the *kefalos* on to the end of your line by wrapping about ten small hooks around half of a long bread roll (apparently the round ones don't work). This hook-ridden lump of bread, known colloquially as *akanthochiros,* the hedgehog, is then cast into the sea from the beach. Usually at this point all or most of it falls off, and to the accompaniment of much commiseration and sympathy from his fellows, the luckless fisherman reels in his line and the *kefalos* gets another free meal.

This small fishing fraternity, consisting of Savvas the Bank, Costas the Leather, Christos the Paint

Instantly hooked a whopper

and Harry the Optimist, spends many happy hours in pursuit of the elusive fish. When one of them eventually hooks a big one, they all rush to help him land it, and the subsequent acts of bravery and guile are talked about for weeks.

One day, with the others all at work, Harry was fishing alone. He hurled his hedgehog far out to sea and instantly hooked a whopper. He reeled it in carefully, for the *kefalos* is notorious for getting itself off the hook. He had it pretty well landed, thrashing about half in and half out of the water, when it freed itself and looked set to disappear back into the sea.

Maybe fishing hasn't been Harry's forté, but he wasn't in the first fifteen for nothing. Grabbing an old vest that he uses for wiping his hands, he dived full-length on to the fish, which weighed about two kilos, and manhandled it ashore. I have seen some weird improvisations made to fishing tackle here, but to the best of my knowledge, this is the first time anyone has caught a fish using a flying rugby tackle. Accustomed they may be to the eccentricities of the English, but Savvas, Christos and Costas are still speechless.

22. PARADISE AT LAST

There is always something in this magic island to capture your interest and imagination. If, like me, you have a love of wildlife, you will find species which enthral you and others which mystify you. From butterflies that dance in the sun to fruit bats that sleep by day in deep, dark caves, the commonplace and the unusual are all here to be observed. Nature has this way of providing all things for all species - some of which work and some of which don't. Predators are camouflaged to fit in with the environment so that their prey doesn't see them coming. Those which tend to become prey themselves, however, are given camouflage so that predators find it hard to see them. Other species affect certain forms of behaviour to guard against those that prey upon them. They haven't worked out how to deal with man's genius for upsetting the applecart yet, though.

In the spring I was watching a line of procession caterpillars crossing the road. I was rather impressed with the action they were taking. They shunted along like a little train - each time one lost contact, the one in front would stop and wait until they all caught up with each other again.

"You see how clever they are?" I said to Harry.

In deep, dark caves

"If they crossed this large open space in ones and twos, they would be picked off by the birds, who are now looking for food by the ton to feed their young. Connected like this, the birds think it is a snake and leave them alone. They can cross quite safely."

With that a lorry drove past and squashed them flat.

Extremely slow creatures, like chameleons, rely on colour changes to disappear from view, while tortoises have a hard shell into which they can withdraw their soft and vulnerable underbody. Other animals rely on speed. We went to the mountain again this year to study and photograph one of the swiftest and most graceful creatures in Cyprus - the *moufflon.* We often see them coming to drink from the dams in the forest behind Argaka and Pomos, but it is extremely difficult to get near enough to be able to photograph them in any detail. However at the forestry station at Stavros-tis-Psokas, deep in the Paphos forest, a small herd of *moufflon* is held captive in a large fenced enclosure within their natural environment.

Dimitris Christofides is the chief forestry officer there. He is also a long-time family friend. When I telephoned him in May, he immediately said he would make arrangements for us to go inside the *moufflon* enclosure. A few days later, dressed as inconspicuously as possible in combat trousers and dark green sweaters, we loaded the camera equipment into the pick-up and headed up the mountain. The early morning sun was just breaking through a layer of high, thin cloud as we came to the end of the tarmac road behind the village of Lyssos. Here we joined the dirt road that would take us up through the forest to Stavros. The track passed through cultivated fields and well-maintained olive groves. Carob trees were still in evidence at this height, and goats thrived in livestock farms situated in the flat-bottomed valley below us. The hedgerows were lush with greenery, and tall, scarlet poppies nodded lazily in the slight breeze among the ripening grasses.

Soon we were into the forest proper and climbing ever upwards. On our left the steep escarpment, thickly clad in pine trees, towered above us while on the other side the ground dropped giddily away into the river-bed far below. The road, hewn out of the mountain, was bordered with slate-like rocks in subtle shades of ochre and brown. Here and there wide streaks of verdigris showed where copper ore was present. A variety of diverse trees and shrubs grew among the pines, while the sweeping terrain was thickly carpeted with pine needles and strewn with wild flowers. Lavender-pink and ivory-cream rock roses bloomed in profusion on either side of the road, and clumps of yellow phlomis provided splashes of bright colour in startling contrast.

At last the long winding climb came to an end and we sat down thankfully at the *kafenion.* The forestry officers greeted us warmly, and as I sipped my coffee, I noticed a tiny *moufflon* poking its head around the kitchen door. Just five weeks old, it appeared to be quite

Just five weeks old

domesticated, though shy. Its mother had given birth by the roadside when snow was thick on the ground - too deep for the new baby to follow her back into the forest. The foresters had kept watch for two or three hours, and when the mother did not return, they had brought it to the station before it could freeze to death. The captive *moufflon* would not accept it, so it had to be hand-reared. The little creature began to thrive. Now, five weeks later, it had the run of the place and was a great tourist attraction.

Andreas Tofouris, one of the forestry workers, held up the key to the cage. He was to be our guide for the morning. As we climbed the steep track around the outside of the wire fence towards the gate, he told us that inside the wire there were three males together with five females and four young. Outside, living wild in the forest, were an estimated two thousand *moufflon.*

Somewhat breathless, we reached a shed at the top where sacks of food for the animals were stored. Once inside, the door was locked behind us and we passed through another doorway out into the large enclosure. There was a dry and sheltered plateau just below the store-shed. Here, on the only level area in the whole place, covered feeding troughs had been set up. In front the ground dropped steeply away into a tree-clad ravine. I looked around for the abseiling ropes, only to see Andreas making his way nimbly down the almost vertical terrain. I took a deep breath and followed him. Loose earth and stones slid away under our feet as we picked our way from rock to rock among the trees and shrubs. *Moufflon* have a strong herding instinct, and they were all together at the lowest point of the enclosure, watching us warily.

Andreas indicated that, once we were settled in a central position, he would go down and drive them up along the side of the fence towards us. Harry set up his cameras and I concealed myself between a couple of large boulders under a tree.

The little herd advanced a few yards and then stood looking from our position towards Andreas and back again - the animals uncertain about the intrusion into their territory. The babies, some with the umbilical cord still adhering, stayed close to their mothers. The largest male was a magnificent creature with patches of white on his flanks. His head, also dusted with white, was crowned with enormous curved horns. His nose twitched as he sniffed the air cautiously. He was beginning to shed his winter coat and the sleek new hide gleamed through in places.

As we watched and photographed, a nightingale burst into full-throated song somewhere nearby and a jay, with its brilliant blue wing flash, came to perch on an overhead branch. The *moufflon* made no sound, but when Andreas moved nearer, the big male whirled and led them, as one, up the side of the mountain and around behind us at an incredible speed.

In the space of a couple of hours, Harry had finished his sketching and had used all his film. We bade our

Watching us warily

hosts farewell and set off on the long journey back down the mountain. As we drove we spoke little - my head was full of images I wanted to describe. I looked at the escarpment on the other side of the gorge for signs of *moufflon* in the wild, but these secretive creatures were hidden somewhere deep in the forest. Here and there water had gushed down towards the river-bed, sweeping trees and top-soil away in its path, and the denuded slopes looked barren and uninviting. Today the reafforestation scheme and careful terracing to stop soil erosion means the future of the primaeval forest looks assured.

It was noon and the overhead sun shone down on bright flowering shrubs bordering the roadside. Butterflies, alighting on like-coloured blooms, rose in clouds like mini bomb-bursts as we passed. There were thousands of them - their delicate and fragile beauty no less captivating than the *moufflon* we had come to see. I gazed out over misty peaks rolling away into the distance, feeling strangely drawn by the timeless quality of the mountain and knowing it would not be long before I returned to this enchanted forest.

* * * * *

In June, flame of the forest trees spread broad feathery green canopies, crowned with scarlet blooms, while densely-flowered jacaranda trees, the colour of bluebells in an English wood, lined the roads. Summer had come.

Royal purple and dark red bougainvillaea sprawled over the house and mature shrubs in the garden flowered in a dazzling array of colours. The last thing I heard at night before I fell asleep was the soft calling of owls, and in the morning I was awakened by the murmuring of doves. It was hot, and as the sun rose, the incessant, pulsing sound of a million cicadas rose to a deafening crescendo. The colloquial name for these creatures is much more fitting. The Cypriots, with their love of that which is both logical and onomatopoeic, call them *ziziros.* I don't mind the noise they make when, in years like this, they appear in such large numbers. It is having to run the gauntlet of them in the garden that I can't stand. Every time I pass close by the trees and shrubs, several of them will suddenly lift off with a shrill squeak and come right at me. As they approach they spray a minute amount of some unspeakable liquid. I have no idea if this is a defence mechanism, a form of attack, or whether they simply suffer from weak bladders. Quite frankly I do not wish to know. Usually they just bump harmlessly away again, but sometimes they get their nasty little legs entangled in my hair and the frantic movement of their wings as they try to free themselves is horrendous. I avoid wearing a low neckline when I go to water the trees, to save having to do a sudden strip-tease if one of them goes down my neck. I also keep the car windows closed driving down our narrow lane, which is bordered by thick shrubbery. It's like passing through a hail of machine-gun bullets as the beastly things fly wildly from one side to the other. You can easily tell when strangers come up the lane in *ziziros* time. Cars come to a sudden halt and the occupants make a quick exit as one or more of these large ugly insects comes in through the open windows.

Eos, Goddess of the Dawn, must have really had it in for her former lover, the handsome prince Tithonus, when she turned him into a cicada.

By the end of the month hundreds of circular drill holes had appeared in the baked earth all over the garden, and the trees and shrubs above were festooned with the desiccated skeleton cases left behind by the cicadas as they emerged in their new form.

The water in the swimming-pool warmed to a pleasing 28 degrees Celsius, and every time we swam, whether by day or by moonlight, we agreed that it had been well worth the traumas we had suffered during its construction. We couldn't face painting it again this year, and with visitors needing to smother themselves in sun-barrier creams, we found that a lot of the oil adhered to the walls in places, discolouring the blue paint.

"I'll put on a snorkel-mask and rub along the bottom chamfer with a sponge," said Harry.

He donned his mask, grabbed a large sponge and disappeared beneath the surface - only to reappear seconds later. He dived down again and the same thing

The desiccated skeleton cases

happened. He stuck his head out of the water.

"I can't stay down there - there's nothing to hang on to. As soon as I use my arm to clean horizontally, I float up again. You'll have to help."

That last sentence is wont to put the fear of God in me. Usually when my help is invoked, a pig's ear of major proportions is in progress. I couldn't quite see what he expected me to do.

"It's simple. You just stand on my back, push me down and keep me there with your weight while I work."

"How will I know when you need to breathe?"

"I can hold my breath for ages. In any case I'll soon let you know, don't worry."

I began to think I might enjoy this.

"You realise you will be completely at my mercy?"

"Huh."

I swung my legs over the edge and placed my feet in the middle of his back.

"That's it. Now you stand on me to get me down, then sit on me to keep me there. You'll have to hang on to the side so that we don't both float away."

I stood on him and he went down like a stone. He began to rub the walls clean while I gripped the edge to steady us. He tapped my ankle and I obligingly moved along a few feet so he could reach the next bit. This was a piece of cake.

He kept tapping my ankle and I had to admire

both the amount he was doing in one go and the length of time he could stay underwater. Suddenly I was violently tipped over as he came up out of the water like a Cruise missile, gasping and whooping for breath.

"What the hell are you trying to do? I'm not a so-and-so fish - I have to breathe now and then, you know."

"You said you'd let me know when you needed to breathe," I replied indignantly.

"I *was* letting you know. I kept on tapping your foot."

The funny side of it all suddenly hit us and we began to laugh. Thereafter, things deteriorated rapidly because we simply couldn't stop laughing. As soon as he went under he'd give a great snort of laughter and I'd be somersaulted off his back again.

"Heaven knows what people will think is going on here," I spluttered. "It's a good job no one can see us..."

Somehow we made our way around the pool, restoring the lovely blue colour to the walls. He made one last effort to finish the final stretch and then erupted beneath me again. When I surfaced, I found myself looking at a couple of complete strangers who were staring anxiously down at us.

"Are you all right?" asked the man. "We thought somebody might be in trouble."

"We're sorry to intrude," added the woman. "The receptionist at the hotel said you would sign these books for us if we came down. We called and rang the bell, but no one answered and then we heard these strange noises."

I don't remember the names of these very nice people, but I'm sure they left thinking we were both completely mad.

Rob and Helen, some close friends of ours, came for lunch. Rob, a marine engineer and scuba-diver, obviously thought so too.

"All you need is a weighted belt to keep you down," he said to Harry. "I'll bring one next time I come."

He did and it works like a dream. It's not half as much fun though, Rob.

I once wrote that one day we were going to live in paradise at the back of beyond. Paradise is a word frequently used by people who step inside our boundary for the very first time. To us it is home, and I never cease to be thankful for whatever fate it was that led us here. It is still high summer as I write this. Dusk is falling and smudged violet shadows are creeping over the mountains. As the light fades, the insistent shrilling of cicadas will die down - to be replaced by the preeping of tree-frogs and the monotonous piping of the little Scops owls. Bats will flit over the pool and small nocturnal creatures will forage for food in the moonlit garden. Pale moonlight, bathing the wild and remote Akamas, will turn the bay into a silver lake. Spellbound as always, I will gaze upon its beauty before I go to bed. Then, with a mind cleared of mundane thoughts, I will drift into a deep and contented sleep beside the man who shares my life.

EPILOGUE

Inexorably the years have moved on, but I have found an inner peace within a sweet and troubled land. This ancient, rugged island grips my heart. Here each day it seems that some small miracle of nature makes my spirit soar and binds me to the natural world. A world of symmetry and balance. Of awe-inspiring power and strength. Of patterns and colours beyond imagination. A world of unimagined tenderness and beauty beyond belief. For who could not be moved to hear the nightingale's lament, or on a dark, deserted beach, see tears roll from a breeding turtle's eyes?

I've heard nightingales that make me weep and owls that will not let me sleep. Frogs that sing in dew-wet trees; the soporific hum of bees.

I've seen herons, in formation, fly across a darkening sky; and snowy egrets skim the waves in streamlined symmetry.

I've seen flocks of pink flamingos flying low across the bay; where white-capped waves, whipped by the wind, carpeted their way.

I've seen a barn-owl take a mouse with moonlight-silvered fur; seen mating snakes dance in the lane and heard the nightjar's churr.

I've held an owlet in my hand, a falcon on my arm. I've tagged a turtle late at night. I've watched an ox-calf born.

I've seen scaly lizards laying eggs; and snakes with blind blue eyes. Chameleons whom camouflage makes masters of disguise.

I've seen huge-eyed, furry fruit bats hanging, upside down, in trees; seen spiders drift on gossamer on jasmine-scented breeze.

I've seen ghost crabs, with their eyes on stalks, hold baby turtles fast; seen foxes, hunting late at night, lope swift and silent past.

I've watched a flying fish rise, iridescent, in the sun; and seen a cormorant dive in the place where it went down.

I've seen dolphins leaping in the wake that streamed beside our boat; a kingfisher that perched on board to slide fish down its throat.

I've watched the sky at sunset turning crimson, rose and

red; and seen cranes, on mass migration, pass in thousands overhead.

I've seen a sky of burnished bronze, a sea of molten gold; and mountains wreathed in milky mist when dawn breaks, pale and cold.

I've sensed the ebb and flow of life throughout the passing years. and on a lonely, moon-washed beach, I've seen the breeding turtles' tears.

Sheila Hawkins
Neo Khorio, 1998